English *for* TRADE FAIRS AND EVENTS

SHORT COURSE SERIES

Britta Landermann
and Jane Maier-Fairclough

Cornelsen

Impressum

Verfasser:	Britta Landermann, Bielefeld
	Jane Maier-Fairclough, Düsseldorf
Berater:	Linda Cox, Wuppertal
	Eleanor Kamtsikis-Jones, Hamburg
Redaktion:	Kathrin Köller
Redaktionelle Mitarbeit:	Oliver Busch (Wortliste), Rani Kumar, Menemsha MacBain, Katrina Walsh
Bildredaktion:	Uta Hübner; finedesign, Berlin
Layout	
und technische Umsetzung:	finedesign, Berlin
Umschlaggestaltung:	Jan Haux, Berlin

Quellen

Illustrationen: Christian Bartz, Berlin: S. 14, S. 22, S. 25, S. 43
Fotos: Titelfoto © iStockphoto: Eduardo Leite; **S. 6** © Corbis: Chat Roberts (u. S. 3, S. 5, S. 57); © iStockphoto: Mark Massel; © iStockphoto: Maartje van Caspel; © iStockphoto: Mark Massel; **S. 7** © Shutterstock: StockLite; **S. 8** © iStockphoto: Stefano Alberti; © iStockphoto: Grzegorz Petrykowski; **S. 9** © iStockphoto: Mark Massel; **S. 10** © Shutterstock: StockLite; **S. 11** © iStockphoto: Aldo Murillo; **S. 12** © Shutterstock: StockLite; **S. 13** © iStockphoto: Artiom Muhaciov; **S. 14** © Corbis: Epoxydude/fstop (u. S. 3, S. 5, S. 57); **S. 16** © Shutterstock: rorem; © Shutterstock: Volkova Anna; © Shutterstock: Africa Studio; © Shutterstock: vovan; **S. 19** © iStockphoto: Andrew Rich; **S. 20** © Shutterstock: Stephen Coburn; © iStockphoto: blufish77; **S. 21** © Getty Images: Marcelo Santos; **S. 22** © iStockphoto: Andrey Artykov (u. S. 3, S. 5, S. 57); © iStockphoto: Troels Graugaard; **S. 24** © iStockphoto: ShutterWorx; **S. 27** © iStockphoto: Steve Debenport; © iStockphoto: Eric Hood; **S. 28** © iStockphoto: Jacob Wackerhausen; © iStockphoto: Abel Mitja Varela; **S. 29** © Getty Images: Paul Thomas; © Shutterstock: Adriano Castelli (2); © Getty Images: Siri Stafford; **S. 30** © Corbis: Zac Macaulay/cultura (u. S. 3, S. 5, S. 57); **S. 31** © iStockphoto: Alex Slobodkin; © iStockphoto: Francisco Romero; **S. 32** © iStockphoto: Troels Graugaard; **S. 33** © iStockphoto: 4x6; © iStockphoto: A-Digit; **S. 36** © iStockphoto: kristian sekulic; **S. 37** © Corbis: Colin Anderson/Blend Images; **S. 38** © Corbis: Hans Bjurling/Johnér Images (u. S. 3, S. 5, S. 57); © iStockphoto: Eduardo Leite; **S. 39** © iStockphoto: Troels Graugaard; **S. 41** © iStockphoto: BlueJeanImages; **S. 42** © iStockphoto: nicolas hansen; **S. 44** © iStockphoto: nicolas hansen; **S. 45** © iStockphoto: nicole waring; © Shutterstock: StockLite; **S. 46** © iStockphoto: R_R (u. S. 3, S. 5, S. 57); © Fotofinder: Maria Irl/imagetrust; © iStockphoto: Stígur Karlsson; **S. 49** © iStockphoto: Abel Mitja Varela; **S. 50** © Shutterstock: auremar; **S. 51** © Shutterstock: Geanina Bechea; **S. 53** © iStockphoto: gehringj; © Fotolia: mars; © iStockphoto: ariwasabi; © Fotolia: Robert Kneschke; © Shutterstock: ImageryMajestic; © iStockphoto: Neustockimages; **S. 54** © Corbis: Redlink (u. S. 3); **S. 55** © Getty Images / Stefania D'Alessandro/Stringer (u. S. 3); © iStockphoto: PixelEmbargo; **S. 56** © iStockphoto: Günay Mutlu (u. S. 3); **S. 58** © iStockphoto: D_A_S_H_U; **S. 60** © iStockphoto: Grzegorz Petrykowski; **S. 62** © iStockphoto: D_A_S_H_U; **S. 72** © iStockphoto: D_A_S_H_U; **S. 76** © iStockphoto: D_A_S_H_U; **S. 81** © iStockphoto: D_A_S_H_U;

www.cornelsen.de

1. Auflage, 1. Druck 2012

Alle Drucke dieser Auflage sind inhaltlich unverändert und können im Unterricht nebeneinander verwendet werden.

© 2012 Cornelsen Verlag, Berlin

Druck: Stürtz GmbH, Würzburg

ISBN 978-3-464-20475-7

 Inhalt gedruckt auf säurefreiem Papier aus nachhaltiger Forstwirtschaft.

Table of contents

Why English for Trade Fairs and Events?

Trade fairs are a hub for valuable information, brand new business ideas, exciting networks and successful top leads.

Trade fairs are also incredibly demanding for exhibitors and attendees who are exposed to a wide range of communicative tasks and are put under a lot of pressure. Being able to deal with business partners in English is often the decisive factor in succeeding at the show.

English for Trade Fairs and Events provides relevant material to prepare students for the show in virtually no time at all. Its collection of practical and ready-to-use resources include:

- A clear, 6-unit structure with relevant topics like booth set-up, customer meetings, networking events, product presentations, lead management and dealing with visitors direct students to the skills they need.

- Easy-to-use interactive exercises with useful phrases and correct technical terms provide an opportunity for practise.

- Simulations and personalized tasks help students activate their own knowledge and make use of their experience.

- An amazing range of accents in the listening tasks, among them Chinese, Italian and Indian, prepare students for the use of English as a lingua franca in the international world of trade fairs and events.

- Real-life case studies allow students to consolidate what they have learned.

- The "Yellow Pages" at the end of the book provide students with a practical toolbox containing phrases for specific purposes.

Let's go for the lead!

Britta Landermann
Jane Maier-Fairclough

Needs analysis

Before being engulfed by the multiple demands in the run-up and during the busy trade fair times, it's always good to consider your personal tasks. This book will prepare you for all the trade fair related tasks you might need to do in English, but first take the time to find out what's most important for you.

Have a look at the list below and tick the skills that you consider important. Which do you want to acquire or improve? Add any that you think are missing.

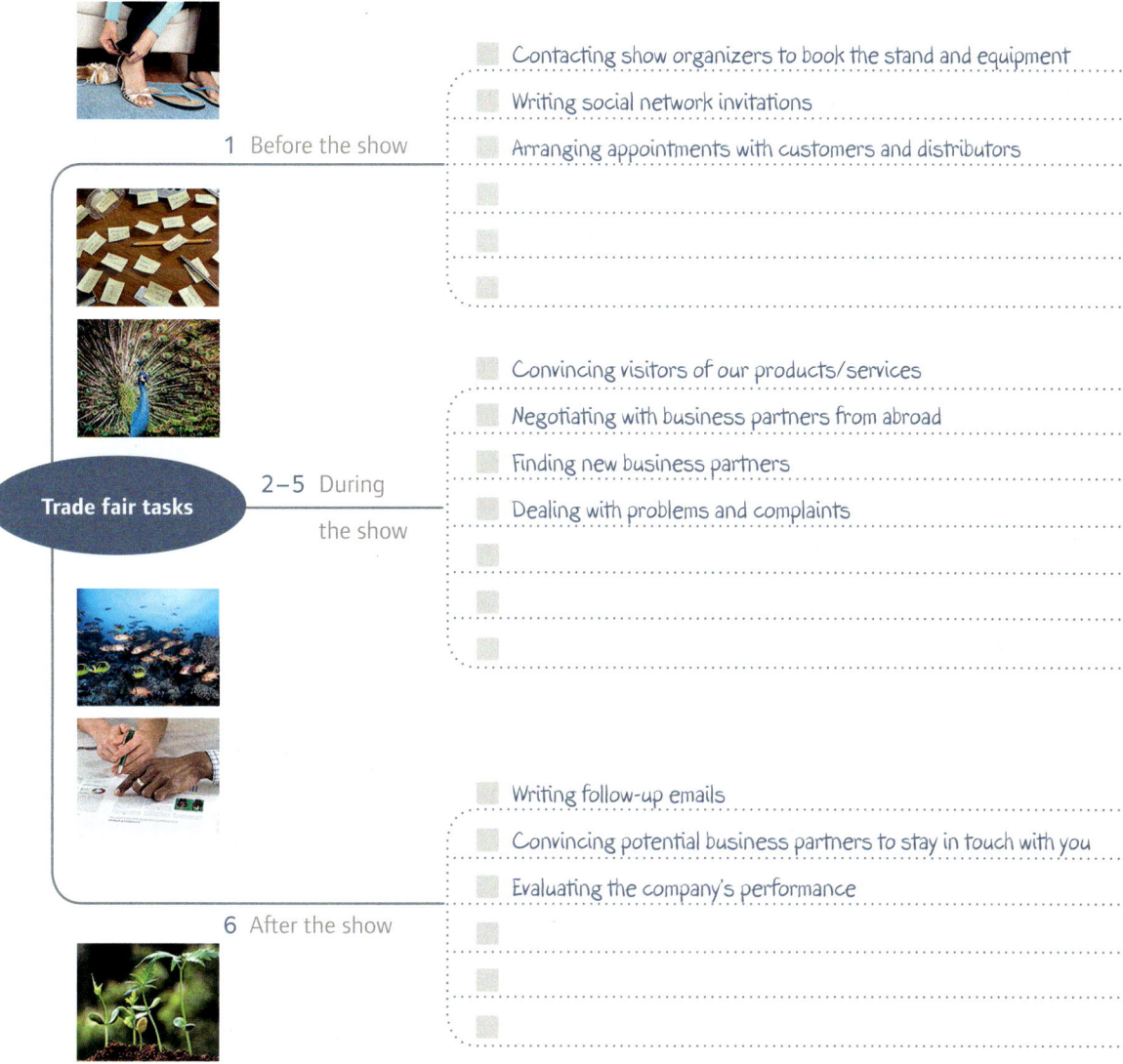

Trade fair tasks

1 Before the show
- Contacting show organizers to book the stand and equipment
- Writing social network invitations
- Arranging appointments with customers and distributors

2–5 During the show
- Convincing visitors of our products/services
- Negotiating with business partners from abroad
- Finding new business partners
- Dealing with problems and complaints

6 After the show
- Writing follow-up emails
- Convincing potential business partners to stay in touch with you
- Evaluating the company's performance

Have a brief look at the objectives at the beginning of each unit to find out where these skills are covered.

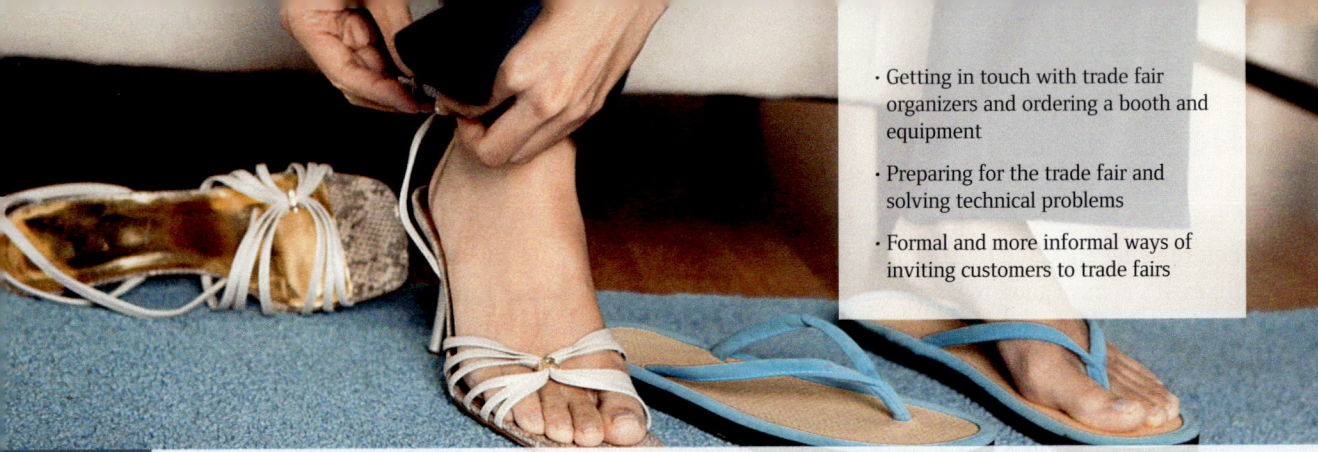

· Getting in touch with trade fair organizers and ordering a booth and equipment

· Preparing for the trade fair and solving technical problems

· Formal and more informal ways of inviting customers to trade fairs

1 Preparing for the Show

🔊 02 **Listen to two employees discussing the pros and cons of attending trade fairs. What issues are they are talking about?**

> Exhibitions and trade fairs are a great way of building customer relations.

> Well, it's all just a big show, isn't it?

How many trade fairs do you attend per year?

What kind of trade fairs do you go to?

What do you consider to be the main advantages and disadvantages of trade fairs?

1 **Look at the website of a trade fair organizer in Birmingham and find synonyms for the words below.**

NTFC National Trade Fair Centre

24-hour help desk
Exhibitor service
Arrival and stay
Calendar

Home
Exhibitors
Visitors
Press
Services
Exhibition grounds
Contact us

With more than 20 interlinking halls, the NTFC is one of the largest venues for your trade fair success in the UK. From international industrial trade fairs to consumer events to niche market trade shows, we have unrivalled experience and resources.

The NTFCs close co-operation with trusted support providers guarantees an incredible trade fair experience in a secure environment – perfectly planned and smoothly run through a single point of contact. Our easily accessible venue can be reached via public transport,

1 attendees   _visitors_   2 competently ....   3 connected ....   4 fair grounds ....

5 reliable ....   6 site ....   7 unmatched ....

Did you know?

The words *trade fair*, *trade show* and *exhibition* are all commonly used when talking about any kind of fair. There are various types of trade fairs if you want to be more specific.

Consumers trade fair Verbrauchermesse   **Leisure trade fair** Freizeitmesse

Industry fair Industriemesse   **Specialized fair** Fachmesse

2 Danil Antonov works as a sales rep for CTMove, a German company specializing in conveyor technology. CTMove has decided to attend a trade fair event in Birmingham this year. Danil's boss has asked him to finalize some details regarding the stand booking.

🔊 03 Listen to Danil phone the trade fair service hotline for exhibitors. Fill in the information on his notepad.

Stand rental	Price per square metre?	1
Stand type	Row, corner, end or island stand?	2
Stand construction	Booth packages available?	3
Stand engineering	Electricity, water and compressed-air connections?	
	....	4
Rental furniture	High tables, shelves, counters?	5
Security services	24 / 7?	6
Logistics	Setting-up time for the stand?	7

3 What you need at the stand. Sort the words below into the correct categories.

additional stand personnel · amplifier · arm chairs · audio equipment · carpet · catering personnel · cleaning staff · computer work stations · data projector · display cases · electricity · flooring · high-speed internet access · hooks · lighting · literature stands · loudspeakers · picture rails · plasma screen · power outlets · promotional staff · racks · security services · shelves · sockets · stools · visitor management · waste management · water

Rental furniture and equipment	
	Services
Presentation technology	
	Technical equipment

4 Complete the NTFC's services website with words from exercise 3.

National Trade Fair Centre

Home
Exhibitors
Visitors
Press
Services
Exhibition grounds
Contact us

It all boils down to planning

Walk on air

No matter which of our stand packages you decide on, we guarantee excellent _flooring_ [1] specially adapted for carrying heavy loads. Hard-wearing .... [2] serve as additional noise reduction and make your visitors feel welcome. Choose among a variety of appealing colours and patterns.

Enough room for your success

High-class rental furniture, like our highly flexible .... [3] and our rack systems store any displays and items you deem necessary. Our plexiglass .... [4] cases protect and make the most of any valuable items you would like to present at your stand.

Security matters

Your success is dear to us. Our 24-hour .... [5] make sure nothing gets lost during your busy trade fair days – or nights. Your dedicated Security Event Manager will provide you with a security package that will meet your specific needs, whether it is security guarding, ticket checking or .... [6] management. Please contact our Security Event Manager for more information.

Prosperous entertaining

Get your hands free for the real business. Our Event Management team are experts in providing outstanding customer service. Our trained and professional .... [7] turn your company into the perfect host so that you can concentrate on maximizing your ROI. Additional stand personnel also includes .... [8] fluent in at least two foreign languages.

Presentation and technical equipment

We want you to wow your audience without having to worry about pointers, cables and high-speed .... [9]. Our dedicated ClicktoGo team is there to cater for all your technical needs. This includes bringing together telephony, network services, video conferencing, as well as inter-web demonstrations and .... [10]. Our state-of-the-art audio equipment provides you with the latest microphone technology that will surely make your voice heard.

5 There are a few things to be clarified at the stand. Look at your profile in the partner files and simulate the situation with a partner.

▷ Partner A, p. 58   ▷ Partner B, p. 60

6 What would be the ideal stand for your company? Draw a rough floorplan of a stand to suit your company's products or services, adding a list of equipment and furnishings you would need. Then present it to the rest of the group.

7 The technical staff at CTMove need some information before going to the trade fair. Danil's colleague Brian Healey has a list of questions.

From: b.healey@CTMove.com
To: d.antonov@CTMove.com
Subject: **Details about next week's trade fair**

Hi Danil,
Just a few questions.

· The new Convey HG7 weighs 2.3 tonnes. Will that cause problems with the flooring?
· Is it possible to drive in through the side gate of Hall 3?
· Is there any over-night cleaning?
· Do we need to bring along extra containers for residual coolants and lubricants?

Thanks,
Brian

> **Vocabulary Assistant**
>
> **coolant** Kühlmittel
> **lubricant** Schmiermittel

Look at the following leaflet Danil has received from the exhibitor services. Then write back to Brian and answer his questions.

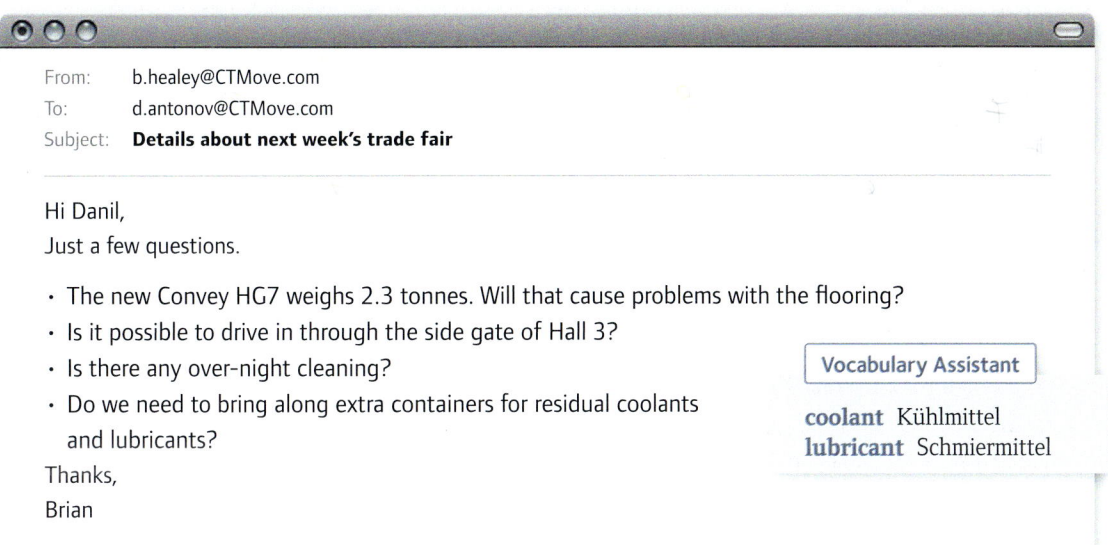

Important Information for Exhibitors

NT
FC

National Trade
Fair Centre

Technical specifications of the indoor exhibition site

Clearance height	12.5m
Maximum floor load	5 tonnes/m^2
Vehicle access, Gate 3	5.5m x 4.5m

Loading and Parking

Loading times	6 a.m. to 1 a.m. daily, see designated loading areas
Parking	Trucks and trailers, Car park 3
	Passenger cars, Car park 4

Please note that a permit is required for free exhibitor parking. The permit can be obtained from the exhibitor's help desk or online at www.NTFC.co.uk/exhibitors/permit.htm

Cleaning Services
Cleaning staff must have access to the stand between 8 p.m and 2 a.m.

Waste Management
Toxic waste (e.g. batteries, lubricants or paint residue) are to be disposed of in the containers between halls 3 and 4. Please note that the CONVEYTECH event management will not be held responsible for any waste left at the stand.

> **Vocabulary Assistant**
>
> **clearance height** lichte Höhe
> **designated** ausgewiesen
> **floor load** (Boden)tragfähigkeit
> **paint residue** Farbreste

Have you ever experienced any problems with loading, restricted building times, or lack of security before a trade fair? Discuss your experiences.

8 Bernard Fletcher, Danil's boss has asked him to draft an email to their main customers to inform them about the trade fair. Read Danil's email and complete the invitation with the phrases from the box.

> 7 look forward to seeing · arrange a personal meeting 8 · be on display for you 3 ·
> 4 particularly excited to be presenting · as one of our valued customers 2 · sign up for 5 ·
> 6 a leading authority on · very pleased to announce 1

From: b.fletcher@CTMove.com
To: Undisclosed recipients
Subject: **CTMove at Conveytech**
Att.: Conveytech ticket
Conveytech Quick Guide Hall 12

Dear "Name"

We are .... [1] that CTMove will be attending the CONVEYTECH at the Birmingham NTFC from 10th – 13th August 2012.

We would be delighted if you, ... ,[2] could join us at this very impressive first-class showcase of state-of-the-art technology created by the world's leading providers of conveyor technology.

Our very latest products and services will .... [3] at our stand and our sales staff are looking forward to answering any of your questions and offering demonstrations on all of the three consecutive fair days.

We are .... [4] our new Convey HG7 at our stand. You can

.... [5] an exclusive demonstration on our website at www.CTMove-Conveytech.com. You will be able to watch the Convey HG7 in action on each day of the trade fair.

The Convey HG7 is an outstanding example of best-practice technology for which we have won this year's Fairfield Innovation Award. The prize will be presented to our company at the CONVEYTECH

by David Lacey, ... [6] the interaction between technology and the people who use it.

In addition, we have attached two complimentary CONVEYTECH tickets which entitle you to enter the exhibition centre on any of the three days on which the fair is taking place.

There is also a map of Hall 12 attached, which is where you'll find our stand, number B78.

We very much .... [7] you at the CONVEYTECH in Birmingham and

please don't forget to .... [8] or demonstration to discuss our new product.

Best regards
Bernard Fletcher

Bernard Fletcher
Head of Marketing
CTMove Headquarters

Vocabulary Assistant

complimentary ticket Freikarte
consecutive fair days aufeinander-
    folgende Messetage
showcase *hier:* Ausstellung
state-of-the-art hochmodern

9 Write an official invitation to your customers using at least five phrases from the box below. Exchange emails with another partner team. Would you accept their invitation?

Useful Phrases

Visit / Join us at …

Our stand / booth is in …

We are particularly excited to be presenting …

… as one of our valued customers …

Inviting customers

We are looking forward to seeing …

Our products will be on display …

We would be pleased / delighted to welcome …

Arrange a personal meeting / demonstration …

10 🔊 04 You will hear a message left on Danil's voicemail. Listen for the following information.

What's the caller's name? 1   Who does he want to meet? 2

When does he want to meet? 3   What's his mobile number? 4

How many complimentary tickets does he request? 5

11 Look at the note Bernard has left for Danil. Write Danil's answer.

> Hi Danil,
> Pls send an email to Arvid. Can't meet him on Aug 10, suggest Aug 11 @ 1:30 pm. Thx. Best, Bernard

12 Bernard invites a customer via a social network to visit him at the trade fair in Birmingham.

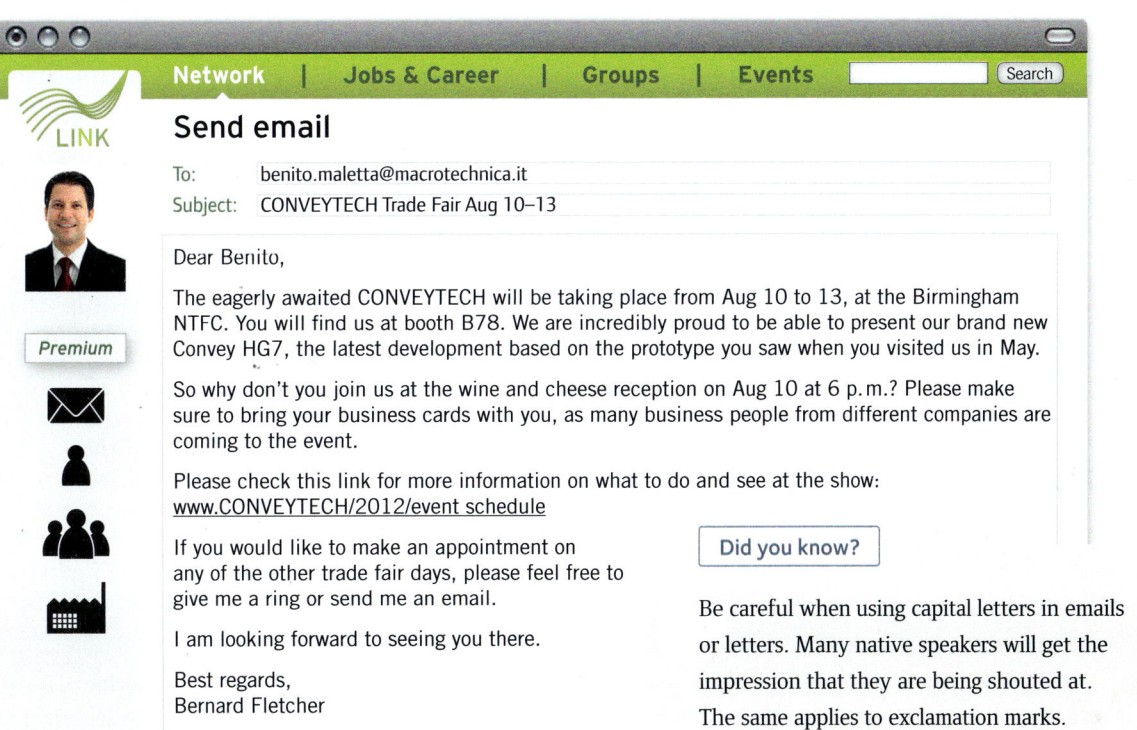

Network | Jobs & Career | Groups | Events | [ ] Search

LINK

Premium

Send email

To: benito.maletta@macrotechnica.it
Subject: CONVEYTECH Trade Fair Aug 10–13

Dear Benito,

The eagerly awaited CONVEYTECH will be taking place from Aug 10 to 13, at the Birmingham NTFC. You will find us at booth B78. We are incredibly proud to be able to present our brand new Convey HG7, the latest development based on the prototype you saw when you visited us in May.

So why don't you join us at the wine and cheese reception on Aug 10 at 6 p.m.? Please make sure to bring your business cards with you, as many business people from different companies are coming to the event.

Please check this link for more information on what to do and see at the show:
www.CONVEYTECH/2012/event schedule

If you would like to make an appointment on any of the other trade fair days, please feel free to give me a ring or send me an email.

I am looking forward to seeing you there.

Best regards,
Bernard Fletcher

Did you know?

Be careful when using capital letters in emails or letters. Many native speakers will get the impression that they are being shouted at. The same applies to exclamation marks.

Look online and find a trade fair which is relevant for your company. Write an informal email invitation to a business partner.

13 ◁ 05 While packing for the fair, Danil discusses the
final checklist with Kelly, an intern from CTMove UK.
Listen to their conversation and write down the items
they are taking. Compare your list with a partner.

........displays...........

....

....

....

Sort the items you noted into the mindmap below. What else would you take? Complete the
mindmap.

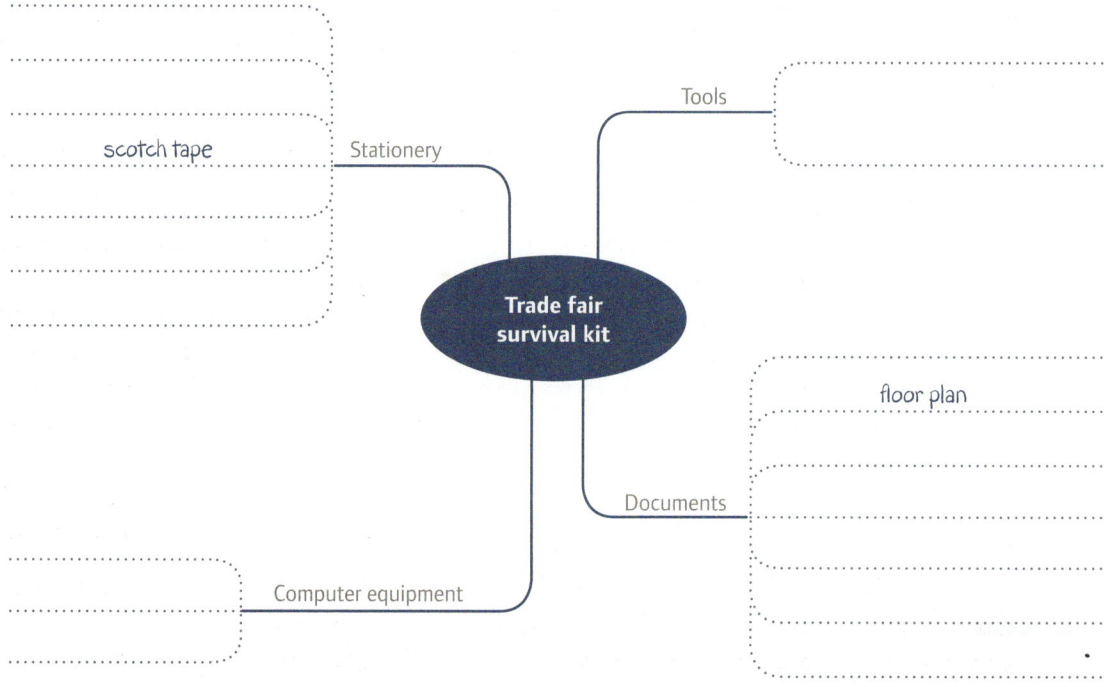

14 ◁ 06 🗂 Listen to the second part of Kelly and Danil's discussion again. Do you use any of the
documents they mention? Which documents do you bring along when visiting a trade fair?

Intercultural Skills

Business cards

Make sure you travel with bilingual business cards. They act as a business passport. In countries where English
is not widely spoken, have your information printed on the reverse side of your cards in the local language.
This is best done in the country you are visiting. Furthermore, be aware of the specific etiquette that exists for
presenting cards, particularly in Asian countries.

For more information go to www.executiveplanet.com.

Trade fairs are a great opportunity to build on a relationship, or destroy it.

There are at least 20 good reasons to attend a trade fair and there seem to be just as many not to. Especially during an economic downturn, many companies tend to cut costs rather than attend costly trade fairs.

5 However, regular trade fair exhibitors insist that it is of the utmost importance to maintain a strong and stable company profile … come rain or shine. This may also be the reason why, according to a survey by the research institute Business and Trade, about half of all exhibitors

10 would rather reduce their stand size and cut training times than pull out of their main industrial fair.

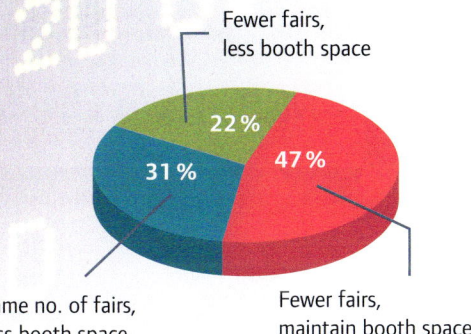

Fewer fairs, less booth space

22 %

47 %

31 %

Same no. of fairs, less booth space

Fewer fairs, maintain booth space

So, what is it we all hope for when preparing for the next show?

"A successful exhibit should help increase sales and gain

15 recognition with our target audience" says Jamie Kelly, CEO of BeltTech, a major belt manufacturer and regular trade fair exhibitor. "ROI is what counts," she adds. "Sometimes, it can be hard for companies to shoulder the additional costs incurred by travel expenses,

20 accommodation, overtime, and staff training."

Business and Trade asked Ms Kelly about what goes on behind the scenes when a trade fair is being planned. Her answer surely reflects many companies' experience: "Well, to be honest, although a lot of money is spent

25 on attending trade fairs, they are often prepared hastily. The preparations have to be made alongside the daily workload. The booth has to be manned taking everybody's holiday arrangements, business trips, language skills, and general availability into account.

30 Promotional material has to be created, translated and distributed well in advance. That's not an easy task."

It seems like there is not much time left for booth staff training.

"My staff knows the products and they know the

35 company. Why should I have to train them?" is a common attitude among many exhibitors. "A lack of staff training can result in countless lost leads. It's like shooting yourself in the foot," warns Sven Bruckner from Train Show, an academy specializing in cross-

40 cultural training for trade show exhibitors.

So, what's the best advice on attending trade fairs when resources are scarce?
"Well, don't go too big and calculate carefully. Always take the time to prepare. It will pay off in the end," says

45 Jamie Kelly. "And," she adds with a smile, "always be ready for the big deal … no matter how much your feet may be hurting."

Over to you

How can trade fairs destroy relationships?
What is your company's attitude towards investing in trade fairs?
How do you prepare for trade fairs? What kind of training do you regard as vital for your trade fair attendance? Does your team have any rules for trade fairs?

- Setting up the stand and sorting out problems
- Arranging appointments
- Addressing different types of visitors appropriately
- Directing people to the meeting point and asking for directions

2   Managing the Stand

"Whatever can go wrong, will."
Have you ever experienced any problems when arriving at a trade fair?

1   Reality strikes. Arriving at the fair and finding out that a lot of things at the booth are not as expected can be a bit of a shock. Sort the words into the categories below.

> broken · clogged · damaged · dim · gone · inadequate · jammed · messy · not connected ·
> poor · soiled · stained · unavailable · unsanitary · unusable

Not clean	filthy		
		out of order	**Not working**
Not to be found	missing		
		weak	**Not enough**

2 Combine the adjectives in exercise 1 with the nouns below to describe problem areas at the stand.

carpet · display · drain · exhibit · extension cord · (fire) extinguisher · hooks · lighting ·
LCD projector · light bulb · lock · locker · picture rails · plug · power outlet ·
rope stanchions · screws · skirted table · outlet · spotlight

Vocabulary Assistant

rope stanchions
Standabsperrungen
skirted table Tisch mit
bodenlanger Tischdecke

I'm afraid the LCD projector is out of order.

We've got damaged picture rails and filthy skirted tables at our stand.

3 In the hectic hours before the opening of the show the adjectives in the sentences below have been mixed up. Find the appropriate adjective for each sentence.

1 The mike you provided is ~~jammed~~. damaged
2 The skirted table is the right size but unfortunately the fabric is **dim**.
3 So much garbage has accumulated in the booth that it is really **damaged**.
4 The drain is **unavailable** and we are afraid the sink is going to overflow.
5 We can't use the lock because it is **unsanitary**.
6 The booth across the aisle is creating a very bad impression because it is so **clogged**.
7 I was hoping the technician could help, but it seems he is **out of order**.
8 We've replaced the spotlights in the display, but the lighting is still very **stained**.

Write three correct sentences using your own word combinations.

4 Read the blog below and choose the correct word or expression from the alternatives given.

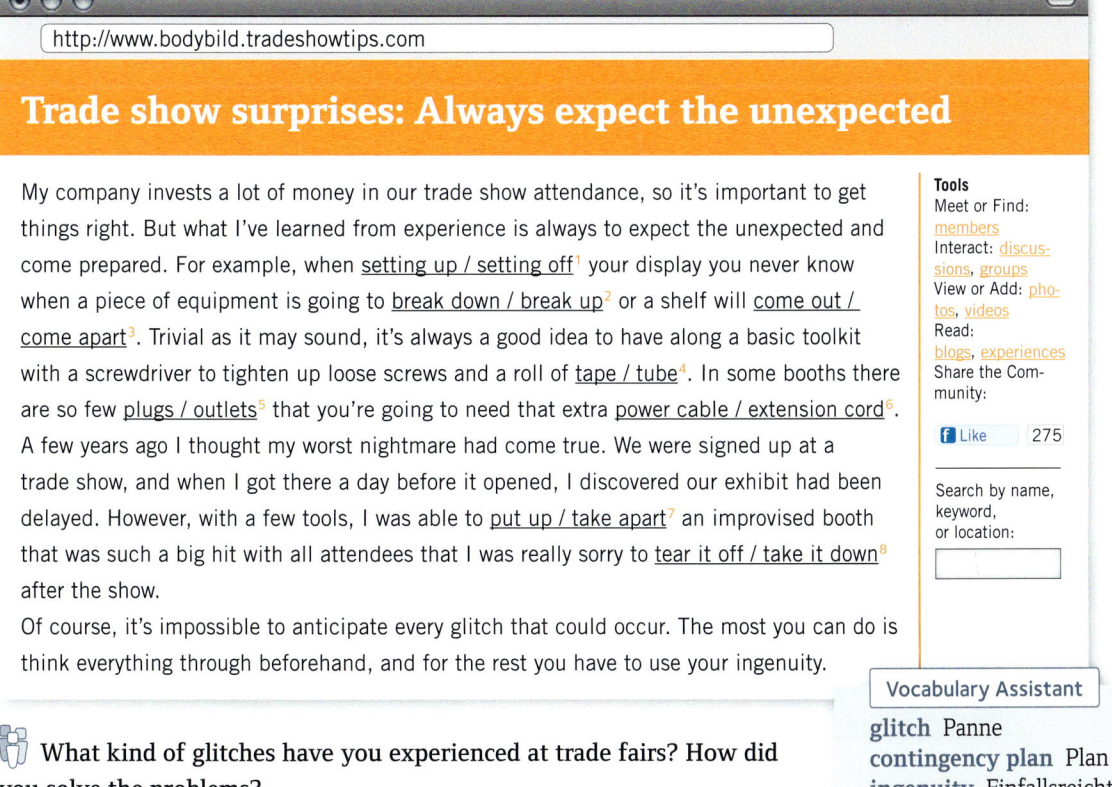

http://www.bodybild.tradeshowtips.com

Trade show surprises: Always expect the unexpected

My company invests a lot of money in our trade show attendance, so it's important to get things right. But what I've learned from experience is always to expect the unexpected and come prepared. For example, when setting up / setting off[1] your display you never know when a piece of equipment is going to break down / break up[2] or a shelf will come out / come apart[3]. Trivial as it may sound, it's always a good idea to have along a basic toolkit with a screwdriver to tighten up loose screws and a roll of tape / tube[4]. In some booths there are so few plugs / outlets[5] that you're going to need that extra power cable / extension cord[6]. A few years ago I thought my worst nightmare had come true. We were signed up at a trade show, and when I got there a day before it opened, I discovered our exhibit had been delayed. However, with a few tools, I was able to put up / take apart[7] an improvised booth that was such a big hit with all attendees that I was really sorry to tear it off / take it down[8] after the show.

Of course, it's impossible to anticipate every glitch that could occur. The most you can do is think everything through beforehand, and for the rest you have to use your ingenuity.

Tools
Meet or Find:
members
Interact: discus-
sions, groups
View or Add: pho-
tos, videos
Read:
blogs, experiences
Share the Com-
munity:

Like 275

Search by name,
keyword,
or location:

What kind of glitches have you experienced at trade fairs? How did you solve the problems?

Vocabulary Assistant

glitch Panne
contingency plan Plan B
ingenuity Einfallsreichtum

5 Write a short blog about the funniest or the most dramatic trade show glitch you have experienced. If possible, use word combinations from the previous exercises.

6 Complete the sentences below with the correct form of the verbs from the box. Notice that some of the sentences require the passive.

> break into · hang up · plug in · set up · shut down · take down · throw away · turn off

1 All light fixtures that have been unplugged during a show must be .... back .... after the show has ended.

2 All exhibit power is permanently .... one hour after the trade show has ended.

3 The organizers require exhibitors to .... all electrical appliances before leaving the booth at night.

4 Thieves .... the exhibition hall last night and stole equipment worth $50,000.

5 We discovered that many attendees .... our brochures during the show, which made us reconsider our advertising strategy.

6 The first thing we always do when arriving at a show is .... our IT equipment.

7 Customer services have promised to send someone to help .... the exhibit when the show is over.

8 If we had more hooks for the picture rails, we'd be able to .... all our posters.

7 ◁07 The following conversations were overheard at trade shows all over the world. Identify the dialogue and the problem in each situation.

1 ◁ Dialogue ▢ : ....

2 ◁ Dialogue ▢ : ....

3 ◁ Dialogue ▢ : ....

4 ◁ Dialogue ▢ : ....

8 ◁07 Sorting things out often depends on using the right language. Match a sentence half on the left with one on the right. Then listen to the dialogues again to check your answers.

1 I'm very concerned	a	a security locker for the night.
2 We were assured	b	about the state of our stand.
3 Would you mind	c	to sort everything out.
4 I'm afraid	d	I don't have that information at the moment.
5 I'd like to recommend	e	that the stand would be cleaned every evening.
6 We'll send somebody over	f	that you move us to a booth with the proper wiring and lighting.
7 We must insist	g	doing that immediately?
8 We're having trouble	h	use a cable to make the connection.
9 I suggest you	i	that you get it in time to set it up for your event.
10 We'll make sure	j	with our wireless Internet connection.

9 Highlight the key phrases in the sentences and sort them into the categories below.

I'm very concerned about the state of our stand.

Making a complaint	I wonder if there's been a mistake / misunderstanding.
	We'd appreciate it if … **Requesting / Demanding help**
Apologizing	I'd like to apologize for the inconvenience.
	We'll send somebody over right away. **Offering a solution / Promising help**

Add other phrases you know to the table.

Sorting out problems at the stand

Partner A

Think of problems you had at a recent trade fair. Imagine you are experiencing them again at your booth at the present trade show. Call exhibitors services to ask for help.

Make sure you use as many of the phrases on page 17 as possible.

Partner B helps out at exhibitors services.

▷ Partner B, p. 58

Trade fair: ....

Company: ....

Problem: ....

Time frame: ....

Intercultural Skills

Personal Space

The personal space people are comfortable with differs from culture to culture, and this fact determines how close you can stand to people when talking to them. For example, North Americans and the British require a lot of space between themselves and the person they are talking to, while Latin Americans, similar to the French and Italians, will stand much closer to their partner in a conversation and may even emphasize what they are saying by touching.

---

10 Choose one of the modal verbs given to complete each of the following sentences. Use the present perfect or the simple past form of the verb.

1 We **should | note** down the serial numbers before leaving headquarters last week.
We should have noted down the serial numbers before leaving headquarters last week.

2 It **must | be** a successful show, as our manager returned with a lot of leads.

3 Unsecured computers **should | never | leave** unattended.

4 The technician **ought to | come** by now. Do you think I should call the Exhibitors Center again?

5 Martin **supposed to | relieve** me at four but he never showed up.

6 She **might | come by** the booth while I'm out to lunch, so I'll leave a message for her.

7 Our booth **supposed to | equip** with eight spot-lights, but only three were delivered.

8 The cleaning staff **should | remove** the trash yesterday, but they didn't.

9 Our display **ought | ship** as early as possible so that it will arrive before the show.

Modal Verbs

Verbs like these show how a speaker feels about a situation:

be supposed to — *must*
can / could — *ought to*
may / might — *shall / should*

In a business context, they are often used like this:

*All electric power **should be shut off** no later than one hour after closing.* (Present simple)
*The doors **ought to have been locked** before the janitor left the building.* (Present perfect)
*It's 10 am now. The display **was supposed to be delivered** at 9:00.* (Past simple)

11 Bodybild is an American company which markets a wide range of fitness products, e.g. treadmills, exercise bikes, and weights, as well as energy drinks and various fitness accessories. They are exhibiting at Wellness Expo in Sydney, Australia.

◁08 Listen and match each of the conversations 1–5 to one of the following situations.

- ☐ a promising business contact wants to arrange a meeting
- ☐ b staff member calls a visitor's attention to information that might interest him
- ☐ c staff member welcomes various visitors
- ☐ d staffer tries to calm an upset visitor
- ☐ e staffer tries to get rid of an annoying visitor

12 ◁08 Listen to the dialogues again and tick the phrases you hear in each category.

Greeting and welcoming
- ☑ Please come in.
- ☐ Hello, how are you today?
- ☐ What can I do for you?
- ☐ Let me know if you need help.
- ☐ I'd be happy to demonstrate our products.
- ☐ Feel free to look around.

Making arrangements
- ☐ When would be a good time for an appointment?
- ☐ Would this afternoon be convenient?
- ☐ How about later in the day?
- ☐ Are you available in the evening?

Turning people away
- ☐ I have another commitment at the moment.
- ☐ Would you mind coming back later?
- ☐ I don't have time to talk just now.

Calming people
- ☐ I can sympathize completely.
- ☐ I understand the problem.
- ☐ I'm confident she wants to see you.

Highlighting information
- ☐ I'd like to point out that we offer discounts.
- ☐ You might be interested in our new range of products.
- ☐ Maybe you'd like to have a look at our new catalogue.

13 At the stand. Read your role card and then work with two other students to play a scene at a trade fair stand. ▷ Stand manager, p. 58   ▷ Visitor 1, p. 60   ▷ Visitor 2, p. 61

Useful Phrases

When you're lost
- I'm sorry I'm running a bit late.
- There seems to be …
- I've (completely) lost my bearings.
- On my left / right there are …
- I'm standing at …
- Could you give me a landmark of some kind?

Giving directions
- Take a left / right into aisle …
- Take the escalator (to) …
- Go straight ahead until you see …
- … just across from …
- We're in the corner booth.
- You're nearly there.

14 ◁09 **Getting your bearings. Listen to the following dialogue and complete the sentences below.**

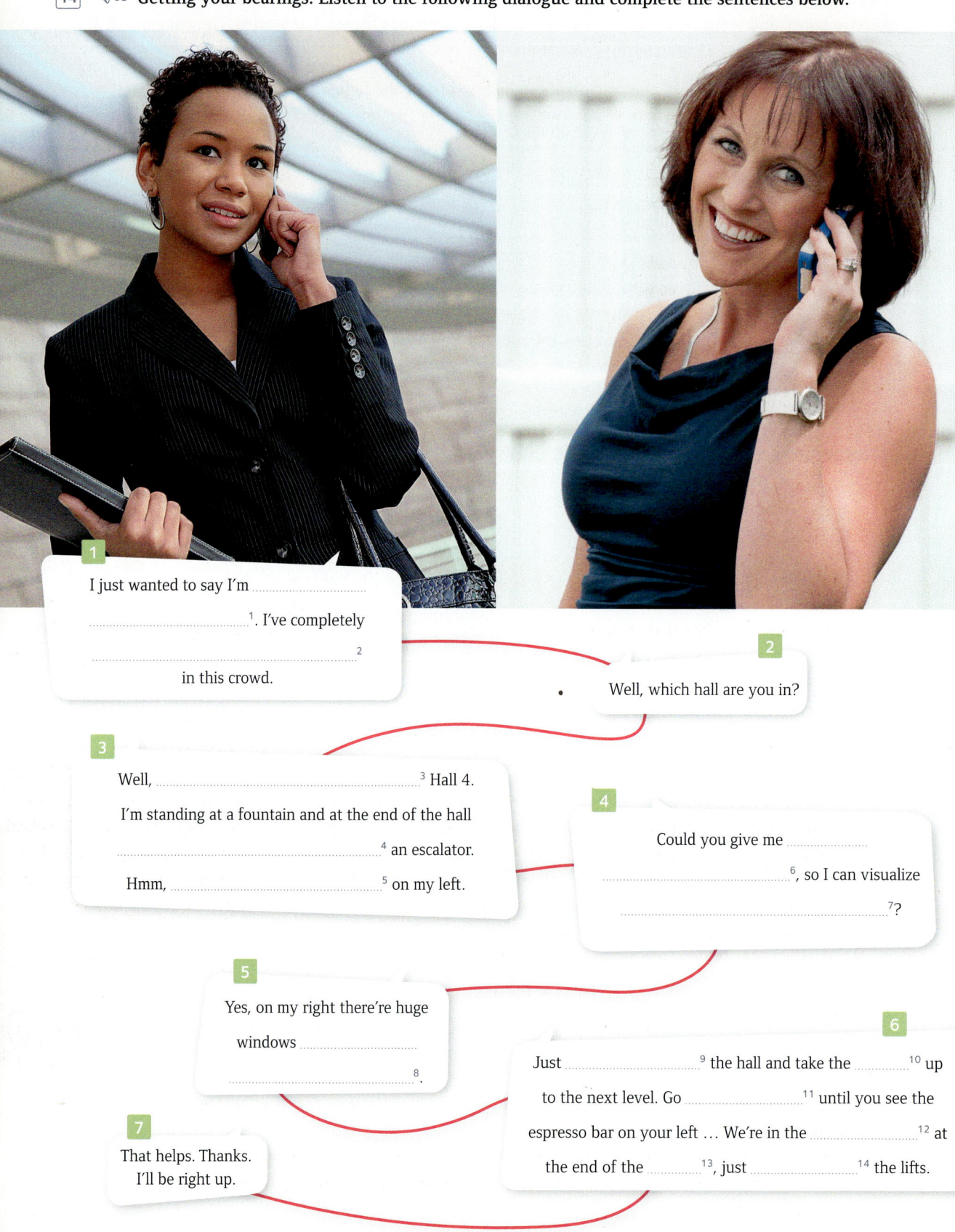

1
I just wanted to say I'm ....
.... [1]. I've completely
.... [2]
in this crowd.

2
Well, which hall are you in?

3
Well, ... [3] Hall 4.
I'm standing at a fountain and at the end of the hall
.... [4] an escalator.
Hmm, ... [5] on my left.

4
Could you give me ....
.... [6], so I can visualize
.... [7]?

5
Yes, on my right there're huge
windows ....
.... [8].

6
Just .... [9] the hall and take the .... [10] up
to the next level. Go .... [11] until you see the
espresso bar on your left … We're in the .... [12] at
the end of the .... [13], just .... [14] the lifts.

7
That helps. Thanks.
I'll be right up.

Fair psychology

There's no better place for broadening your knowledge of human psychology than a booth at a trade fair. This is where you can encounter a wide range of characters.

You'll recognize the *Freebie Freaks* by the bags they're
5 carrying, already stuffed with giveaways from your competitors' stands but not so full there won't be a place for whatever free samples these visitors can coax out of you.

The *Undercover Agent* has a more serious mission. He
10 or she works for your competitor and has come to see what you have to offer that they don't. They're happy to collect the latest brochures and catalogues and engage you in conversation about your state-of-the-art products.

15 The *Vendor*, on the other hand, has come to interest you in his company's product or services, while the *Entertainment Junkie* hangs around booths offering any kind of demonstration or video display. And finally, there is the *Playboy* or *Playgirl*, who is tired of spend-
20 ing evenings alone in the hotel and on the lookout for a companion to while away the hours away from home.

Professor Susan Wheaton from Ashton Business School has good advice for all trade fair exhibitors. "A trade fair is a big investment, so you want to make the most
25 of it. It's important for your staffers to engage as many attendees as possible and ask the questions that will permit them to sort the casual visitors from the ones who are seriously interested in your product. This is called qualifying your leads. If it's done properly, you
30 can soon identify the hot leads – that is to say, the people with the influence and buying power to become big customers."

Jack Kelly of InterCorp tells a story about the casual conversation he once struck up with a very low-key
35 visitor. "This guy looked so unremarkable that he could have been the janitor. But after fifteen minutes' conversation I discovered he had operations all over the world and represented a $6 m sales opportunity. I would never have been able to identify him as an important
40 prospect if I hadn't learned to ask the right questions!"

Over to you

What in your experience is the best way of dealing with each type of visitor mentioned?
Can you think of other typical stand visitors?
How do you make sure you have enough time and space for serious visitors?
What are the 'right questions' to ask to find out whether you are talking to a potentially important prospect?

· Promoting products and services at the stand

· Giving presentations at the fair

· Describing trends and explaining charts in presentations

3 Demonstrating and Presenting at the Show

◁ 10 Claire Laurent from ParlezVous, a French telecommunication company, is talking to two employees from other stands. They are discussing booth design and ways of attracting visitors to the stand. Listen to their conversation. What strategies do they mention?

How do you interest visitors in your products?
What do you think of the "old buddy" strategy? Would you use it yourself?
Discuss strategies for attracting people to your stand.
Can you act out a particularly successful strategy?

1 ◁ 11 Claire is a member of ParlezVous' sales team. Listen to the conversation Claire has at their booth and complete the phrases below.

1 Is there anything you are .... in that I can help you ....?

2 The .... is that it is easy-to-handle and .... weighs 26 grams.

3 This is a point where we are .... to compromise.

4 This will give you .... our terms and conditions.

5 Mr Legrange would be .... discuss a tailor-made solution with you.

6 But .... you what we could do. Why don't I .... your contact details?

7 I'm sure we'll be able .... a solution.

2 🔊11 **Listen to Claire's conversation at the ParlezVous booth again and find good word partnerships for product descriptions.**

1	optimal	a	development
2	competitive	b	device
3	comfortable	c	technology
4	stylish	d	solution
5	sophisticated	e	comfort
6	comprehensive	f	fit
7	latest	g	range of products
8	maximum	h	prices
9	state-of-the-art	i	functionality
10	tailor-made	j	headset

3 **Complete the phrases in the box below so that they are true for you.**

Useful Phrases

We actually specialize in ....
....

This is our latest range of ....

It provides you with ....
....

The .... was a revolution.

There are three things I'm particularly excited about with the ....
....

Promoting Products

It's a unique opportunity to
....

It will make a great addition to your
....

It comes in ....
....

This is an exciting new
....

The beauty of it is ....

Simulation

👥 **Presentation Battle**

With a partner, think of a product you make or a service you offer, and the industry it belongs to. Give it a name and write all the benefits you can think of on your card. Then prepare a presentation and convince your audience of the quality of your product or your service. Collect points for every word partnership and promotion phrase you use.

Product / Service: ....
....

Industry: ....
....

Name: ....

Benefits: ....
....
....
....

4 Claire has signed up for a presentation by Lan Song from Netspeak, a telecommunications company with a neighboring stand at the IT Linked World.

◁ 12 **Listen to Lan's presentation and tick the phrases you hear.**

Workshop 2

Tue, Jun 4, 2:30–3:30,
Exhibition Room 3

Keynote speaker
Lan Song | Netspeak

Where are we headed next? – The Future of Telecommunications

☐ I'd like to apologize for my bad German.
☐ I feel ashamed for having to do this in English.

☐ What I'd like to talk to you about …
☐ What I want to discuss with you is …

☐ I think we all agree …
☐ I believe we can all agree …

☐ Let me talk you through …
☐ Let me give you an idea of what I will be talking about.

☐ Firstly, I'd like to highlight …
☐ First of all, I'd like to draw your attention to …

☐ Fire away.
☐ Go ahead.

☐ What I meant was …
☐ What I was saying was …

☐ To put it in a nutshell, …
☐ What this all boils down to is …

5 Sort the phrases from exercise 4 into the mindmap.

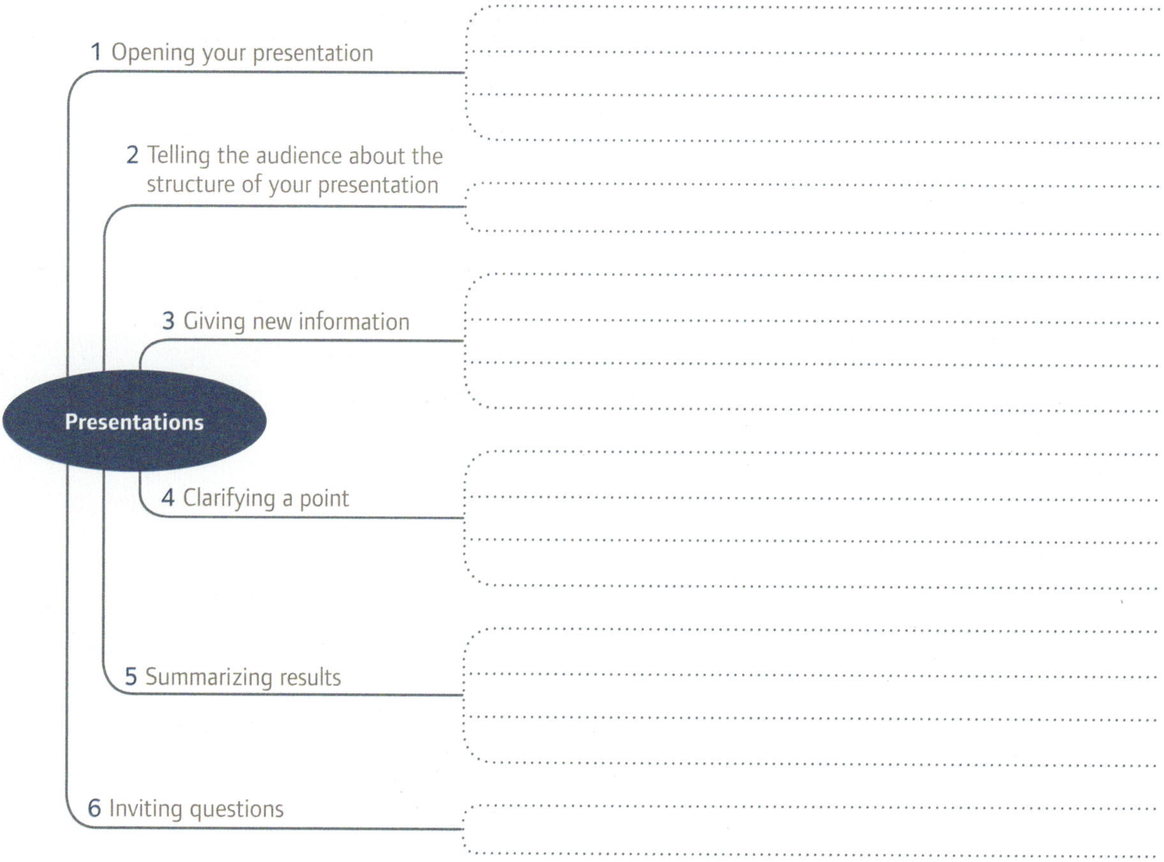

1 Opening your presentation

2 Telling the audience about the structure of your presentation

3 Giving new information

Presentations

4 Clarifying a point

5 Summarizing results

6 Inviting questions

Compare your results with a partner. Add other phrases that you find helpful.

6 Give a presentation about your company and your products or services to a partner. Use the phrases in exercise 5 to help you. ▷ Partner A, p. 58 ▷ Partner B, p. 60

7 Look at the business magazine headlines. Which of the highlighted words describe upward, which describe downward movements and which words describe stable trends? Complete the table below.

Soaring hopes: India – the world's new centre for trade fairs?

Inflation surging to an all-time high

339,000 visitors! CEBIT expectations exceeded.

Düsseldorf and Paris on the same level says fashion show organizer.

Frankfurt Trade Fair experiencing a slump – Berlin on the rise.

Rocketing stand costs make exhibitors think …

Trade Fair Services plc. hit a new low.

Referral marketing gaining in importance.

Share prices reaching a peak.

Prices levelling out. But at what price?

Decrease in android phone prices causes run on mobile phone shops

Economic figures decline

go up rocket increase		
remain stable		
go down plummet decrease by … % fall		

Add other words you know for describing trends and come up with some headlines yourself.

8 Look at one of Lan Son's presentation slides. Use words from exercise 7 to complete her presentation notes below.

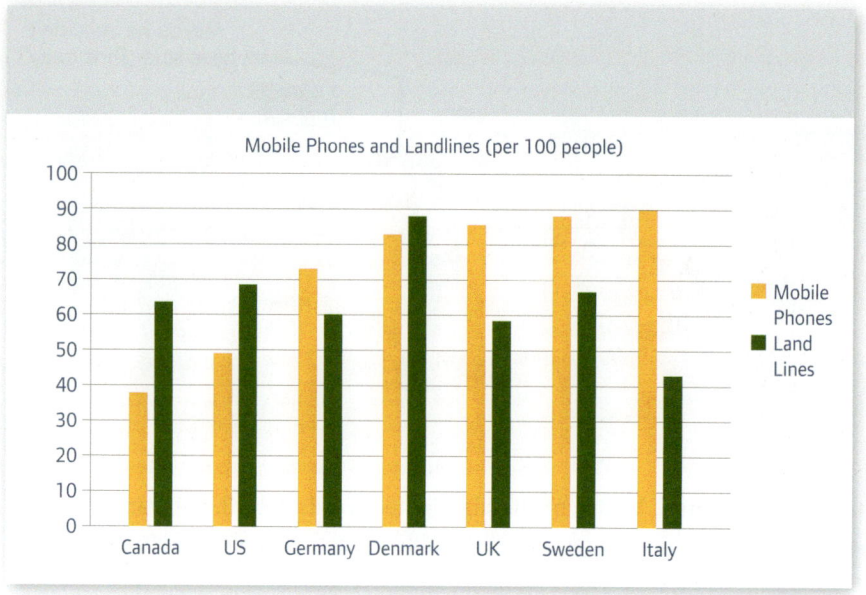

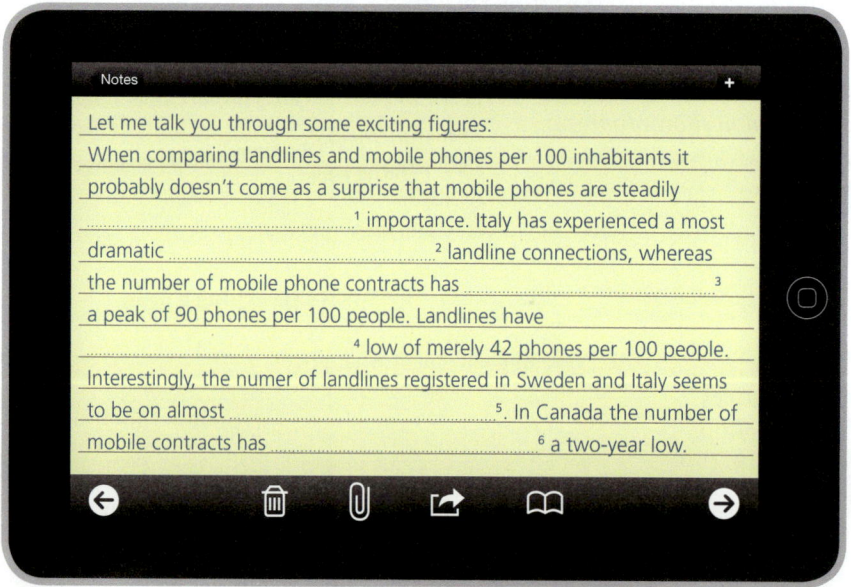

Notes +

Let me talk you through some exciting figures:
When comparing landlines and mobile phones per 100 inhabitants it
probably doesn't come as a surprise that mobile phones are steadily
................................[1] importance. Italy has experienced a most
dramatic ....[2] landline connections, whereas
the number of mobile phone contracts has ....[3]
a peak of 90 phones per 100 people. Landlines have
................................[4] low of merely 42 phones per 100 people.
Interestingly, the numer of landlines registered in Sweden and Italy seems
to be on almost ....[5]. In Canada the number of
mobile contracts has ....[6] a two-year low.

9 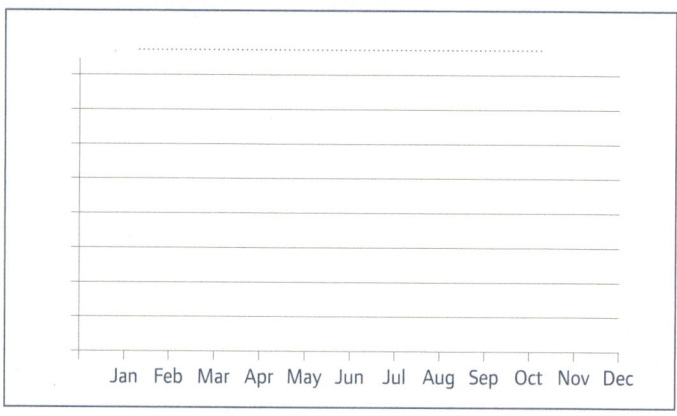 Peaks and Slumps: Describe the chart at the back of the book to a partner. Complete the template on the right following your partner's description.

▷ Partner A, p. 60
▷ Partner B, p. 59

10 Read the interview with Laura Henley, CEO of the consulting agency Trade & Trend. Fill in the missing prepositions.

Interviewer *So, Laura, you're optimistic when it comes to trade show attendance?*

Laura Yes, absolutely, Greg. Despite the economic downturn, trade show attendance in the manufacturing industry has only decreased ....¹ 7 %, although at some trade show locations there has been a rise ....² booth costs ....³ up to 23 %.
Still, 85 % ....⁴ all decision makers say that trade show attendance saves company time and money.

Interviewer *What if you had a crystal ball? What do you think the future holds for trade fairs?*

Laura I think there can be no doubt that social networks are going to revolutionize the way we do business. Visitors now have access to many communication channels. At online trade fairs such as expolearning.com exhibitors meet their visitors virtually and arrange follow-up meetings via social networks. This is already happening. ....⁵ 10 bn, the number of social network accounts outnumber the world's population. Social networks are now turning into business networks.

Interviewer *You are talking about networks such as Facebook and Linked-In?*

Laura Yes, indeed. My company polled about 500 small and medium-sized business owners in 2012 ....⁶ which 75 % plan to make social networking a larger part of their marketing mix in 2013. Six ....⁷ ten decision makers say that social networking has already served to boost sales and revenue. 83 % will devote 11 % or more of their marketing resources to social networking in the new year.

11 Look at the information below and compare the figures with your own experience. Look at these exhibition statistics. Do the figures reflect your own experience?

Trades and Trends

Trade Fair Issues

Booth staffers

24 % speak two languages

65 % speak only one language

11 % speak three or more languages

You would have thought that in the world we live in today everybody speaks at least some English. However, while promotional staff is often fluent in a number of languages, the experts international customers want to talk to frequently lack language competence.

Exhibitors

20 % send customized invitations prior to trade fair

42 % send no invitations prior to trade fair

28 % send standardized invitations to customers

About 40 out of 100 exhibitors do not invite clients to visit their stand at the trade fair. To be honest, I find this a little bizarre. With social media it has become so easy to get in touch with prospective customers all over the world.

Exhibitors

72 % have no formalized lead management

17 % have lead plan but don't really follow it

11 % have efficient lead plan and stick to it

> Almost three quarters of all exhibitors don't have any standardised lead management. I have to admit, I was also lost before we were offered extra training on this.

> I can see whether a stand visitor is really interested in our product even before I've talked to them. It's the way they walk and how they try to make or avoid eye contact.

90% of trade show attendees subconsciously decide whether they will buy from an exhibitor within the first 10 seconds of entering their stands.

Present some of your own trade fair facts and fiction in numbers.

Intercultural Skills

Don't assume.

If the world were a village of 1,000 people, it would include: 584 Asians, 124 Africans, 95 Europeans, 84 Latin Americans, 52 North Americans, six Australians and New Zealanders, and 55 people from the former Soviet republics. They would speak more than 200 languages and reflect an astounding mix of different cultures. Now imagine giving a presentation to that group of 1,000 people.*

Well, this may seem like taking things too far, but actually this is what could happen to you in today's globalized trade fair world. Your presentation success no longer depends solely on your technical expertise or your language skills. Many intangible factors influence communication with your potential business partners when presenting abroad. There are gender-related issues, differences in body language, concepts of time, and differences in the way people show agreement and disagreement. Always bear in mind that how and what you perceive is a reflection of your own cultural values.

So, how can we make sure everybody's standards are met? The answer is: by embracing this diversity, by preparing where we can. What would you assume if your business partner reclined in his chair and closed his eyes while listening to your presentation? That he is tired? That your presentation has lulled him to sleep? If he is from Japan, he may simply use this kind of body language to show he is concentrating.

The solution as well as the difficulty lies in trying not to make any assumptions. Premature assumptions block the way to successful communication.

* from: http://totalcommunicator.com/vol2_2/interaudience.html

Presenting 4 success

Over to you

What is it that makes you remember a company and their products or services?

How important is a good show? What are the standards and expectations in your industry?

Are there any ways of presenting that you wouldn't consider appropriate?

- Initiating a conversation and liaising with potential business partners
- Marketing yourself using positioning statements
- Writing invitations to networking events
- Dealing with difficult stand visitors

Which of the comments below reflect your attitude towards networking?

Networking with business contacts broadens my network and also enhances my social life.

Some people are introverts and don't like making small talk. Networking is just not for them.

All of this talk about networking is a lot of hype. Most networking does not lead to any serious business, but is more about wining and dining …

Cross-cultural networking is usually very time-consuming and doesn't produce much in the way of results.

Business is 80 % networking.

Today you can't do any serious networking without using social media such as Twitter and Facebook.

What are your networking strategies at trade fairs?
What works well? What doesn't?
How would you define networking?

1 ◁ 13 **Listen to a talk given at a pre-show workshop on networking at EarthTech, a trade show for waste management technology held in San Diego, U.S.A. How does the workshop facilitator try to provoke his audience and what objections come from the participants?**

Then choose the right words to complete the following sentences from the dialogue.

1 So before we start, I'd like to pick your **brains | memory | pockets**.
2 If ten of those people turn out to be really reliable long-term business contacts, then that will have a huge **influence | impact** on our sales.
3 I'm looking at this show as an opportunity to establish new **cross-industry | inter-industry** networks and develop synergies among major decision- **managers | makers** in waste management.
4 For me it's all about breaking new **ground | ice**. At the show I want to find out about new market **sections | segments** that could potentially be interesting for us.

2 ◁ 14 Now listen to the workshop facilitator outlining his pre-show networking workshop and complete the list of the topics he will deal with.

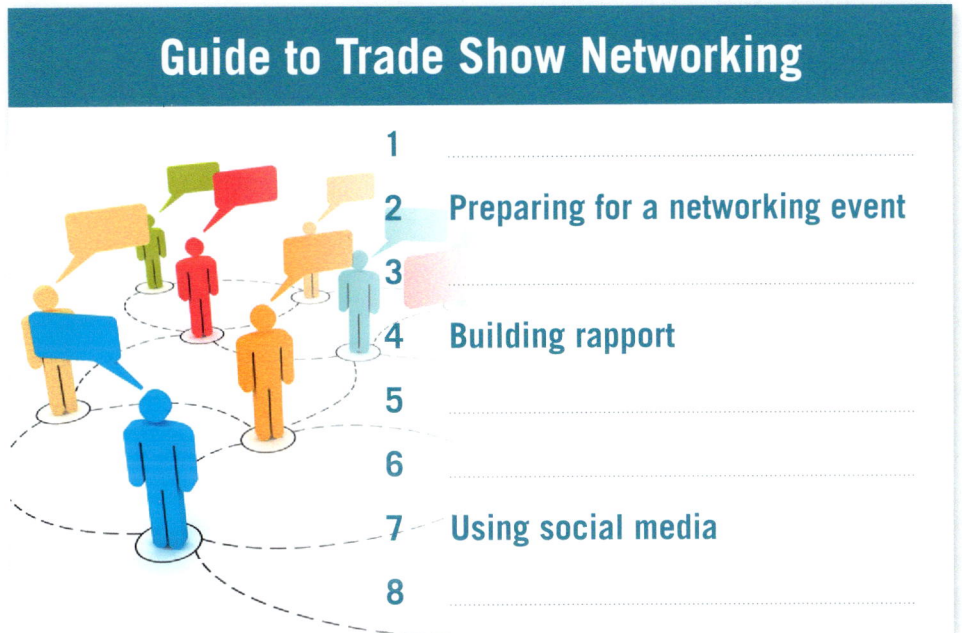

Guide to Trade Show Networking

1 ....
2 **Preparing for a networking event**
3 ....
4 **Building rapport**
5 ....
6 ....
7 **Using social media**
8 ....

Are there any other important networking issues you would have included in the workshop?

3 Complete the following invitation to a networking event with the words from the box.

confirm your participation · dedicated to · drawn from · hosting · in conjunction with · invitees · views

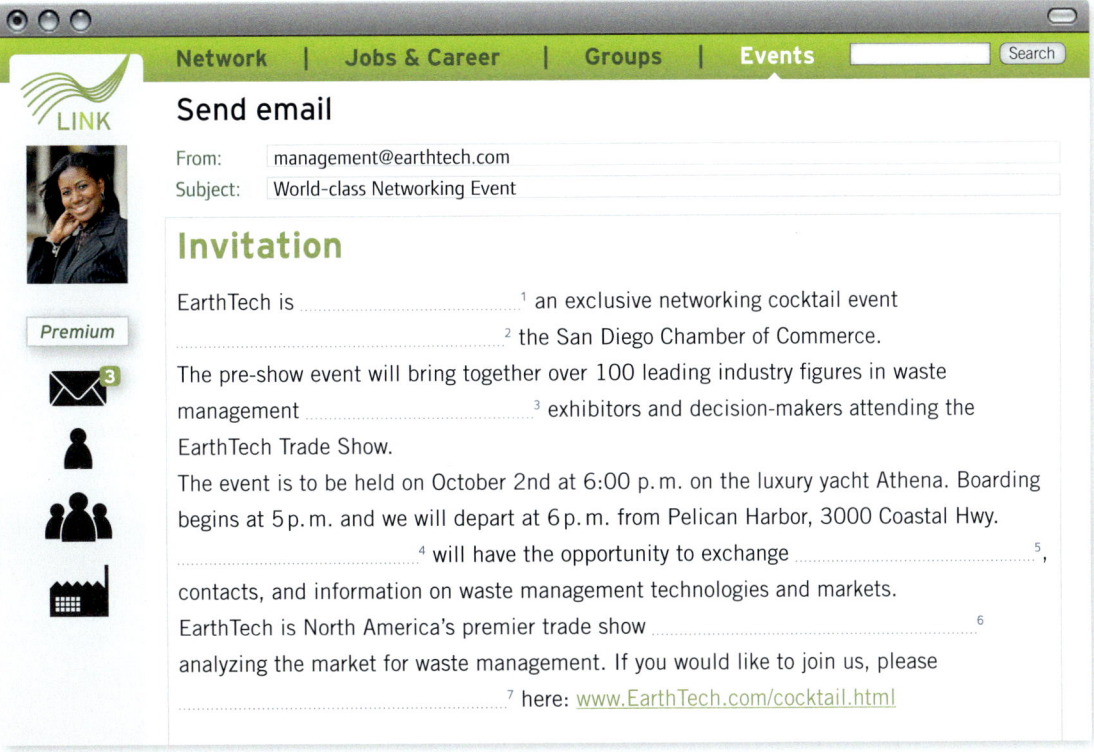

| Network | Jobs & Career | Groups | Events | | Search |

Send email

From: management@earthtech.com
Subject: World-class Networking Event

Invitation

EarthTech is ....¹ an exclusive networking cocktail event
..............................² the San Diego Chamber of Commerce.
The pre-show event will bring together over 100 leading industry figures in waste
management ....³ exhibitors and decision-makers attending the
EarthTech Trade Show.
The event is to be held on October 2nd at 6:00 p.m. on the luxury yacht Athena. Boarding
begins at 5 p.m. and we will depart at 6 p.m. from Pelican Harbor, 3000 Coastal Hwy.
..............................⁴ will have the opportunity to exchange ....⁵,
contacts, and information on waste management technologies and markets.
EarthTech is North America's premier trade show ....⁶
analyzing the market for waste management. If you would like to join us, please
..............................⁷ here: www.EarthTech.com/cocktail.html

Premium

4 With a partner agree on a networking event you would like to invite your customers or clients to. Then write an invitation using phrases from the box or other useful phrases from the EarthTech invitation and your own experience.

Visit / Join us at …

(The event) is to be held on …

(The event) will bring together …

Inviting customers to events

We would be pleased / delighted to welcome you to …

We are particularly excited to be (present)ing …

(You) will have the opportunity to …

We are looking forward to (see)ing you …

You can sign up for …

---

5 🔊 15 The following conversation takes place at EarthTech's networking event. Look at the prompts below. Then listen to the conversation and write down the appropriate responses.

1   Do you mind if I join you?

....

2   Choosing the yacht as a venue was really a stroke of genius, wasn't it?

....

3   You were in the networking workshop a couple of days ago, weren't you? ....

....

4   This is our Sales Manager for the U.S., Steve Macintyre. ....

5   Do you happen to have a card? ....

6   How about getting together later in the show? ....

....

---

6 🔊 16 The words in the following statements are scrambled. Unscramble them, writing each on the correct line according to its function in the positioning statement on page 33. Then, listen to Monika's statement again to check your answers.

1   due to | to offer | design | a | patented | able | unique | features | we're | these
2   our | maintenance | valued | for | clean | their | and | easy | compactors | handling | are
3   and | commercial | we | restaurants | primarily | serve | construction sites
4   near | is | company | its | German | ComPress | with | Stuttgart | a | headquarters
5   wide | compactor containers | to | we | range | a | one-unit models | make | from | breakaway compactors | of | huge

Name and location of the company	
Type of product	
Target customer	
Key benefit	
Reason you can deliver that benefit	

Positioning Statements

A positioning statement is a short statement describing your company and defining the benefit your product or service offers the consumer. It typically contains:

- the name of your company
- the type of product
- the target customer
- the key benefit
- the reason you can deliver that benefit

It might be a good idea to prepare one or two sentences for each point so that you won't have to look for words while you're networking. But remember to keep it short and natural.

Create a positioning statement for your company or for a company you know using the structure above. Try to commit the statement to memory. Then find a partner, so that each of you can practice your positioning statement.

7 In their conversation, Monika and Doug use tag questions to be polite and invite responses. Rephrase the following sentences using tag questions.

Tag Questions

*Maestro is exhibiting in Hall 4, **isn't it?***
*We met at last year's show, **didn't we?***
*Next year I should register earlier, **shouldn't I?***
*You don't happen to have a pen, **do you?***

1 If I'm not mistaken, we met last year.
  We met last year, didn't we?
2 Is it possible you work for Whizz?
3 I think the booths are well equipped. What do you think?
4 Am I right in thinking that we're meeting the new agent this evening?
5 Ken will be at the stand tomorrow. Is that right?
6 She works for our major competitor. What do you know about that?
7 Just wanted to be sure that we've arranged to meet this evening.

Initiate a conversation and try to keep it going as long as possible. Use tag questions whenever you feel they are appropriate.

1 It's a great hotel for conferences, isn't it?

2 It certainly is. Very conveniently located. And they do a great breakfast buffet, don't they?

3 Absolutely. I'm already looking forward to dinner this evening.

4 Oh, the bus to the conference center hasn't left yet, has it?

5 No, it's still waiting over there. You can catch it if you hurry.

Initiating a conversation

With a partner, decide on the kind of product you make and the name and location of your company. Give yourself a name and a position in the company and fill in all the information on your role card.

Then imagine that the two of you are taking part in a pre-show cocktail reception in your industry. You are eager to meet people and make contacts. Act out the situation with another pair, making use of opening phrases, positioning statements and tag questions.

Company: ....
....
Location: ....
Name: ....
Position in company: ....
....
Product: ....
....
....
....

Useful Phrases

Initiating phrases

Do you mind if …

I see you're from …

Let me give you …

I couldn't help noticing that …

I'd like to introduce …

Is anyone sitting here?

So what exactly does … do?

That's very impressive.

I didn't get …

Pleased to meet you.

Responses

I'd love to!

That's a coincidence!

Do you happen to have a card?

How about getting together …

8 ◁ 17 **Steve Macintyre has a visitor at the ComPress stand at the EarthTech Trade Show. Listen and complete Steve's lines with phrases from the box below.**

And so you have an interest in · I see you've been watching ·
If I understand you correctly · So where exactly are you from · Would you mind repeating that, please? ·
So, we're talking about · Maybe you could give me some more details

1 .... our video demonstration. Maybe you have some questions I could answer.

2 ...., if I may ask?

3 .... compactors?

4 ...., you're looking for a solution to your trash and garbage problem.

5 ...., so that we can get an idea of your needs.

6 .... I'm not very familiar with India.

7 .... at least 11 outlets with a daily traffic of over 250,000 customers.

9 Look again at the phrases Steve used in his conversation with Mr. Gupta and sort them according to their function. Add other phrases you know.

....

....

Opening the conversation

Eliciting information

....

....

....

....

Avoiding misunderstandings

10 ◁ 18 You are going to hear remarks made by four different visitors to your stand. Decide which of the functions given in exercise 9 is involved and then find an appropriate response to each visitor.

11 ◁ 19 Monika addresses a visitor to the ComPress stand. Listen to their conversation and decide whether the statements below are true or false.

		True	False
1	The visitor has come to enquire about a specific product.	☐	☐
2	The visitor provides Monika with details about his company.	☐	☐
3	Monika and the visitor agree to meet for lunch.	☐	☐
4	Monika offers the visitor a catalogue.	☐	☐
5	The visitor refuses to give Monika his card.	☐	☐

Listen to their conversation again. What language does the visitor use to avoid answering Monika's questions? Add his phrases to the box below.

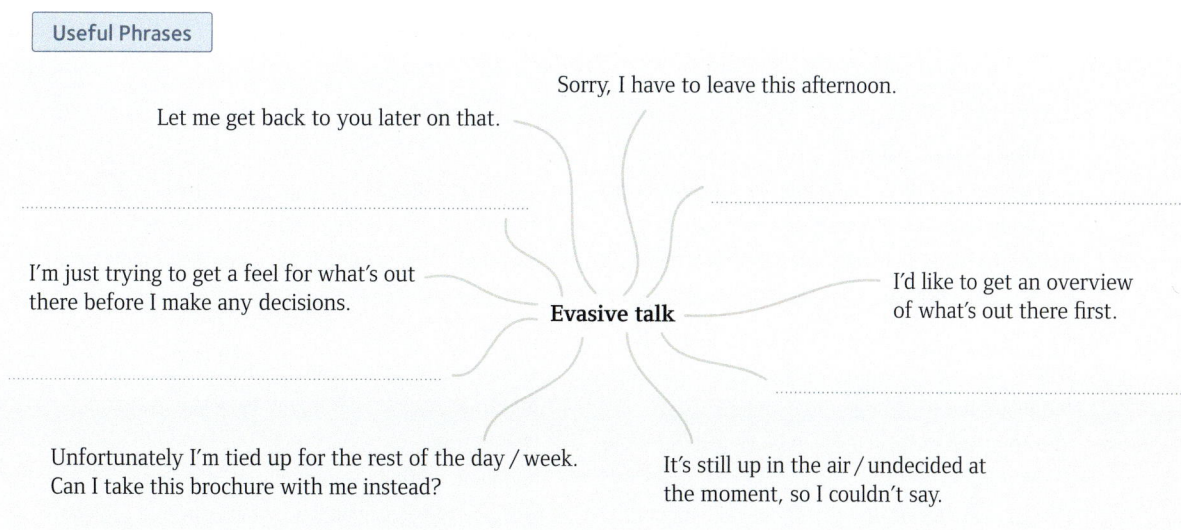

Useful Phrases

Sorry, I have to leave this afternoon.

Let me get back to you later on that.

I'm just trying to get a feel for what's out there before I make any decisions.

Evasive talk

I'd like to get an overview of what's out there first.

Unfortunately I'm tied up for the rest of the day / week. Can I take this brochure with me instead?

It's still up in the air / undecided at the moment, so I couldn't say.

12 What do you think? How would you go about approaching a competitor's stand?

13 Practicing evasive language. What would you say in these situations? Think of your own experiences, then choose one or two scenarios and act them out with a partner.

1 At another stand somebody asks you if you're interested in a particular feature of a product, but you don't want a detailed presentation.
2 You are being asked by a sales rep about the company you work for but you don't want to disclose its identity.
3 Another exhibitor asks you a question about company policy you don't want to answer.
4 A pushy visitor suggests that you make an appointment but you'd rather not.

> **Vocabulary Assistant**
>
> **company policy** Leitlinien des Unternehmens

14 🔊 20 Steve and Monika are having lunch with Mr. Gupta and his nephew Dr. Ashok Gupta, a business consultant living in the U.S. Listen to their conversation and tick the intercultural obstacles that you can detect. Then sort them into the order they appear in.

☐☐ Marriage customs

☐☐ Position / role of women

☐☐ Attitudes towards time (punctuality, etc.)

☐☐ Dietary restrictions due to religious beliefs

☐☐ Dealing with hospitality

☐☐ Significance of family ties

What strategies do the four employ to iron out their intercultural faux pas?

> **Intercultural Skills**

Getting the ball rolling

It has been said that small talk is like a game of tennis. Sometimes it's necessary to serve several times before the game can really start and then the players want to keep the ball rolling as long as possible. It's a kind of game that German business people may regard as a necessary preliminary to doing business but might not really enjoy.

The approach to small talk can be very different in other cultures. British stand reps, for example, tend to approach visitors and quickly engage them in conversation rather than wait for them to approach the stand.

Indian business people regard relationships as paramount and indulge in lengthy small talk before any meeting. They enjoy talking about politics and may be remarkably well informed about events in Western countries.

Whatever culture you are dealing with, it is important to remember that it may have values that differ widely from yours. Accepting this fact with an open mind and finding common ground for conversation will lead to good small talk, which can well provide the foundation for a successful business deal and a long-standing business partnership.

Virtual trade shows – a model for the future

Remember your last trade show – how you spent thousands of company dollars to cart heavy equipment hundreds of miles to the trade show venue? How you spent hours of your precious manage-
5 rial time at the booth, hoping for that sensational lead? And the nights away from home in an expensive hotel room?

That may soon be a thing of the past. Live trade show events are now being challenged by vir-
10 tual gatherings, organized by companies which use state-of-the-art software and technologies such as webcasting, online chats, video streaming, webinars and avatar graphics. Users of the most sophisticated programs can stroll through an
15 online convention center, "visiting" booths and accessing information about the products on offer by a simple click. Sales reps can be contacted for an online chat. Seminars are delivered via podcasts and Webinar platforms.

20 Virtual trade show sites even provide attendees with lounges and cafés, where networking can take place almost like in the real world.

Not only does this represent a sizeable saving on travel costs, other expenses, and the drain on
25 managers' time and energy, it also results in a smaller environmental footprint.

But even though experts estimate the market for virtual show organizers at around $120 million, there are still business people who have trouble
30 saying goodbye to the world of handshakes and cocktail receptions. Virtual shows are not going to replace live events tomorrow. At present, they are providing an interesting complement to real-world shows, especially for 'boutique' gatherings, where
35 it is hard to predict how many people will attend.

What is clear is that in a time of economic uncertainty and rapid technological innovation virtual trade shows have a very promising future.

Over to you

What advantages of virtual trade fairs are mentioned in the article?
What disadvantages do you see to this kind of event?
Would you agree with the statement that networking can just as easily take place in
  a virtual environment?

- Analyzing cross-cultural impediments to business
- Discussing business opportunities with new contacts
- Sorting out problems with suppliers and distributors
- Discussing possible licensing agreements

5 Talking Shop

Rank the following trade fair objectives in order of their importance to you (1–8).

- ☐ Setting up new distribution networks
- ☐ Getting an overview of the competition
- ☐ Recruiting new license partners
- ☐ Meeting business partners to discuss the latest developments
- ☐ Exploring foreign market opportunities
- ☐ Finding new suppliers
- ☐ Discovering new distribution channels
- ☐ Doing market research

Compare your ratings. What other goals does your company want to achieve?

1 In a seminar on international trade fair success, Serge Brenner, Darius Miller and Inga Bergström focus on cross-cultural challenges. Read the following article from their course material.

Learning the cross-cultural ropes

"We were out of our element," says Lisa Hauge from SwedFlow when describing her first experience within the Chinese market. "Chinese authorities seemed to favor local companies and it was very difficult to get in touch with suppliers or sales people directly. The regulatory interferences were more or less unpredictable to us."

5 "Only when we decided to work with Yao Ming, now our agent on site, did the situation improve." Ms Hauge's statement seems to mirror the experience many Europeans apparently have when trying to set up business in China. "You definitely need local help to deal with the red tape involved, the legal requirements and last but not least language and cross-cultural issues," recommends Ms Hauge.

However, the situation for European business people in the whole of Asia-Pacific is improving
10 constantly. "The momentum in the region may continue. Recently leaders of the Asia-Pacific Economic Cooperation (APEC) launched an initiative aimed at making it easier for small and medium-size companies to do business through systematic peer learning and assistance across economies."

Vocabulary Assistant

peer learning Wissensaustausch unter Kollegen
regulatory interferences behördliche / staatliche Eingriffe

2 Find the right synonyms for the highlighted words in the magazine article on page 38.

1 Apart from financial and cross-cultural worries, you may also have to face legal **problems**.

issues

2 A lot of difficulties are simply **unforeseeable**.

3 Chinese authorities seem to **prefer** local businesses.

4 Everything changed once we got support from a **local** agent.

5 The hardest thing is to deal with all the **bureaucracy**.

6 The reports in the ChinaBiz forum **reflect** many Europeans' experience.

7 It's not easy to **contact** other providers directly.

Compare Lisa Hauge's experience with the situation for business start-ups in Germany. Is Germany a red tape country? What recommendations would you give?

3 ◁ 21 **Listen to Serge, Darius, and Inga discussing their various experiences. Which cross-cultural issues do they mention?**

> **Vocabulary Assistant**
>
> **not to be able to make head or tail of something** aus etwas nicht klug werden
> **things run like clockwork** die Dinge laufen wie am Schnürchen

4 Complete the following sentences so that they are true for you.

1 Dealing with red tape can be

2 To explore new distribution channels is

3 The fastest-growing market for my company is

4 We have manufacturing sites in , because

5 Adherence to deadlines can be

6 It's best to deal with the legal jungle by

7 Taking part in cross-cultural training is

Compare your sentences with a partner.

Does your company do a lot of international business? Have you experienced any problems due to cross-cultural issues? Which of the experiences Inga, Serge, and Darius mentioned in their discussion have you already had?

5 Gärtner Life GmbH, a family company based in Germany with subsidiaries in a number of European countries, would now like to test the Chinese market for sales. They have contacted Luan Zhang from China Ware about a possible cooperation.

Gärtner Life GmbH
Household Appliances and Cookware

Thomas Baker
Sales Manager

www.gaertner-life.de

Mühlenstraße 14–18
67655 Kaiserslautern
Office   +49(0)631 590 17
Mobile   +49(0)1631 590 172
Email   t.baker@gaertner-life.de

Read the email CEO Oliver Lücke has quickly jotted down to sales manager, Thomas Baker. Then, help Thomas find more formal words so that the email can be forwarded to the sales managers of the other Gärtner branches. Use the words in the box to replace the informal expressions.

---

accelerate / advance · contact · cooperate with · create / form · focus on · gain ·
keep sb. informed · maintain · participate · reduce

From: o.luecke@gaertner-life.de
To: t.baker@gaertner-life.de

Hello Thomas,

Thanks for the sales report for Q1. Great job. Although the figures don't look that bad, I think we have to cut down on labor costs and make new market segments. My feeling is that we should speed things up with China Ware. They're also taking part in the Home Living Trade Fair in April.

Please get in touch with Luan Zhang to make an appointment. The agenda should include the following:
• Exploration of market opportunities: What chances does the market offer?
  Should we mainly check out the Zhejiang area?
• Quality Management system – How can we make sure European quality
  and safety standards are kept?
• Sales team: Is there a trained sales team, sales support?
• Can we work together with regional distributors?
• What are the territorial restrictions?
• Would China Ware be interested in setting up a strategic partnership?

You may want to ask Rita Gao to join you for the talk.
Please keep me in the loop.

Thanks,
Oliver

Oliver Lücke I CEO Gärtner Life GmbH I Mühlenstraße 14–18 I 67655 Kaiserslautern I www.gaertner-life.de

Would you change anything else to make this email more appropriate for the other sales managers?

6 Look at Bernd Lücke's email again and find verbs that can be used with the nouns below. Add at least one more verb you know.

.... quality standards

.... explore .... market
opportunities ....

.... regional
distributors

.... manufacturing
site .... strategic
partnership

.... sales team .... quality management system

Write an email to Luan Zhang asking him for a meeting at the HomeLiving Trade Fair.

7 How do you prepare for intercultural meetings? Where do you get the necessary information? Work in groups and present your findings in class.

> **Intercultural Skills**

> **Guanxi: Doing business in China**
> China is a huge country with hundreds of dialects and ethnic groups. As a result, there is no recipe for how best to do business in China. However, there are a couple of things one needs to consider: Guanxi is "the fundamental glue that holds society together." Getting the right people to connect you to other business people is essential to Chinese business culture, which is very much based on trust. Personal contacts should be cultivated and fostered through invitations and business dinners.

8 🔊 22 Thomas Baker and his colleague Rita Gao meet Luan Zhang at the China Ware stand. Listen to the beginning of the meeting between Gärtner and China Ware and jot down the phrases they use to welcome each other and exchange pleasantries.

> **Vocabulary Assistant**
>
> **be tied up** beschäftigt sein
> **diligent** fleißig, sorgfältig
> **HKETO** *Hong Kong Economic and Trade Office*

9 How do you think their conversation will end? Do you think Thomas will manage to maintain China Ware's interest in Gärtner Life?

10 ◁ 23 Thomas and Rita continue their conversation with China Ware. Follow them through the various stages of their meeting. Tick the phrases you hear.

		P	S
▢	We would be particularly interested in …	▢	▢
▢	I'm convinced that …	▢	▢
▢	As you probably know …	▢	▢
▢	What I was thinking of …	▢	▢
▢	Could you imagine …	▢	▢
▢	What I actually had in mind …	▢	▢
▢	We would like to focus on …	▢	▢
▢	May I propose that …	▢	▢
▢	We would be more than delighted …	▢	▢
▢	May I present you with …	▢	▢
▢	We would like to give you a gift …	▢	▢
▢	We would appreciate that.	▢	▢
▢	It has been a real pleasure …	▢	▢

> **Did you know?**
>
> The word *appreciate* is often used to express gratitude or understanding.
>
> I **appreciated** the good services the fair provided.
>
> While we **appreciate** that many cultures have different notions of time, this does not make arranging meetings easy.
>
> You will **no doubt appreciate** the fact that our labor costs are very high.

◁ 23 Mark the phrases in exercise 9 according to the category they belong to. Are Thomas and Rita exchanging pleasantries (P) or making suggestions (S)? If necessary, listen to the conversation again.

11 👥 Practice making suggestions and answering politely.

▷ Partner A, p. 59   ▷ Partner B, p. 61

▷ Partner A, p. 59   ▷ Partner B, p. 61

12 ◁ 24 There is more business going on at the Gärtner Life booth. Listen to a meeting with the representative of Frigotón, David Gomez. What are the issues in this conversation?

Look at the situations below. What would you say? Use phrases from the conversation between Thomas Baker and David Gomez. Brainstorm additional phrases as a class.

1 You would like to start discussing business.   *Shall we move on to business?*

2 You want to ask a question about somebody's business situation.

3 You would like to know the reason why something happened.

4 You would like to communicate that you understand the other's point of view.

5 You want to hear the other person's proposals.

6 You want to express agreement.

13 ◁ 25 Listen to another meeting between Rita Gao and Ewa Pajak from Warsaw White Goods, the Gärtner distributor for Poland and Belarus. The two enterprises have been business partners for years. What are the issues in this conversation?

Did you know?

Did you know that many English speakers tend to use the word *issue* when talking about a *problem*? They might also talk about *open issues*.

Now match the following sentence parts from the dialogue.

1	Would you mind if	a	we had agreed on that during our last meeting.
2	Is there anything I could do	b	with the trade fair displays.
3	I fully understand	c	we started 15 minutes earlier?
4	I was under the impression that	d	and get back to you within 2 days.
5	I will certainly sort this out	e	to enhance the communication flow?
6	You mentioned certain issues	f	that this must have been very annoying.

Did you know?

Be careful when answering the question *Would you mind if …?* The answer should usually be *no*.

Would you mind if *we met 15 minutes later?* **No, of course not.**
Would you mind if *we met 15 minutes later?* **Well, actually I would.** *I've got another meeting in half an hour.*

14 Make the sentences in the discussion below more appropriate. If necessary listen to track 25 again.

1 This campaign is a disaster.

2 I have better things to do than to waste my time in this meeting.

3 Really, you've made a complete mess out of this!

4 So, what's all this fuss about?

5 I have to talk to you about this again.

6 I can try to find a solution when I have the time.

15 Cultural awareness. Are you aware of your own cultural standards? Would you consider yourself unbiased? Business Partner A and Business Partner B have arranged a meeting at a trade fair. Appoint one observer whose job it is to monitor the interaction.

▷ Business Partner A, p. 61   ▷ Business Partner B, p. 59   ▷ Observer, p. 61

16 What are the main benefits of working with faraway business partners in other countries?

17 🔊 26 Thomas Baker has one last meeting, this time with Gianna Bertani from Italy. Ms Bertani's company, Squisito, specializes in state-of-the-art espresso machines. Gärtner Life is interested in gaining her as a license partner for their high-quality range of espresso machines. What are Ms Bertani's main preconceptions?

🔊 26 Now listen to their conversation again and complete the sentences below.

1 I have to .... we are really proud of this espresso machine.

2 Our main .... are baristas and gourmet coffee shops.

3 However, we think that with Vivacita we would be able to ....

4 Our contract with Couleur Café is not going to .... before the end of 2015.

5 .... we were thinking of …

6 But as I said, you will find Gärtner Life a very .... partner.

7 Why don't we sit down and .... of a possible

licensing agreement from then? Mr Falke could send you ....

Useful Phrases

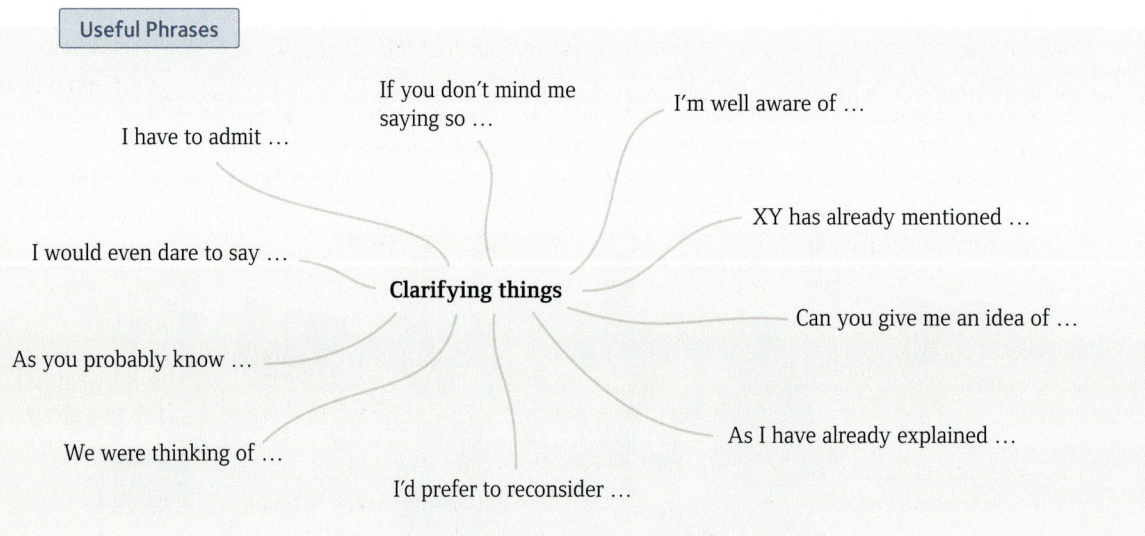

I have to admit …

If you don't mind me saying so …

I'm well aware of …

I would even dare to say …

XY has already mentioned …

Clarifying things

As you probably know …

Can you give me an idea of …

We were thinking of …

As I have already explained …

I'd prefer to reconsider …

---

18 Match the definitions (1–5) with the licensing terms (a–e) Thomas Baker and Gianna Bertani use in their conversation.

1 numbers of days from the commencement of an agreement to its completion

2 prepayment in anticipation of sales

3 portfolio or set of products

4 unique license

5 percent of the income from the sales of a product

a royalties
b exclusive rights
c contract period
d range of products
e advance payments

cross cultural business

Collaborating with German management – help needed

fusionmonkey

Hello everybody, I'm new to this forum. My company is based in Nancy in France. We had a meeting with some guys from our German subsidiary
5 last week. The plan was to discuss a possible standardization of our warehouse management systems. Well, as I said that was the plan ... But I have to say these Germans really blew the whole thing. They turned up with a 20-page report on what could be done and when and what they would not need from us. I mean it felt like our input was actually not needed anymore. My whole team was kind of
10 frustrated. Can anybody help? I'd really like to get things going again.

6 hours ago | 3 comments

Lost in meetings

Curt07

Hi guys, I'm from Germany and I work for a German telecommunications company. I could do with some help re a business meeting I had with a
5 Singapore company we had established contact with at the Franchising and Licensing Fair. The whole cooperation didn't really work out well ... I had been under the impression that we were there to finally sign the contracts we had been discussing during the trade fair and two weeks after. Instead I found myself confronted by three employees who surprised me with various suggestions about how
10 the contract could be changed for the better. And they kept a voice recorder running during the meeting. When I found out that the decision-maker would not even turn up I was so angry that I interrupted the meeting and left the room to call headquarters ... Fortunately, somebody from HQ managed to make a new appointment.

Can somebody help me with what went wrong? What should I have done?

15 8 hours ago | 6 comments

ccb staff member

Hi Curt07

Thanks for sharing this. Actually, your experience is really nothing unusual. Business people in Singapore tend to regard meetings as
20 something very flexible. Contracts are there to be revised and adapted. So, you shouldn't be surprised if the decision-makers don't turn up for every meeting. It might help if you try to focus less on the signature than on the process itself ... If you need further info, check out www.executiveplanet.com.

Over to you

What do you think went wrong?
What advice could you give fusionmonkey?
Continue the blog.

• Staying in touch with business partners
• Following up with contacts by email and telephone
• Issuing follow-up invitations and keeping contacts interested
• Evaluating trade fair experiences

6 Following up on the Show

What happens after the show? How do you follow up on an event?

What measures do you take during the show to make sure you get the most out of the contacts you have made?

Match the verbs with the nouns to describe what happens after a show.

1	check	a	booth
2	complete	b	exhibit
3	debrief	c	follow-up emails
4	develop	d	forms
5	dismantle	e	headquarters
6	qualify	f	leads
7	report back to	g	newsletter
8	send	h	prospects
9	take down	i	report
10	visit	j	staff
11	write up	k	stocks

1   **Read the following three emails (A–C) and answer the questions below.**

1   Which email requires a prompt answer?
2   Which email gives the recipient the impression that the writer is empowered to make decisions?
3   Which email suggests that a decision must be taken?
4   Which email will the writer probably follow up with a telephone call?
5   Which email shows the supplier is willing to go out of his way to satisfy the customer's requirements?
6   How does email A give the recipient the feeling that the sales manager remembers him personally?

A

Dear Mr Sharma

I just wanted to let you know that it was a pleasure meeting you at our stand at the Home Living Trade Fair in Frankfurt last week and hearing about your expansion plans into the mobile eating branch. As I mentioned in Frankfurt, I find your plans concerning new mini-coffee bars at train stations around the U.K. very interesting.

I am going to be in your area the week after next and thought that we could take the opportunity to meet. If you have time, I could give you a quick personal demonstration of the coffee machines more suited to your plans. I still have a couple of slots free on Wednesday and Friday but, of course, I could easily reschedule to meet you on another date if that is more convenient. I also wanted to mention that we could discuss the colors and designs of suitable machines to match your company image if you are interested.

I have attached our latest catalogue and price list as promised, as well as a list of discounts, including the ones for new customers. Of course, if you are interested in having the coffee machines customized, we would have to talk about the price per unit, as this would depend on the quantity you order.

I look forward to hearing from you and hope I can be of service to you.

B

Dear Mr Zhang

It was a great pleasure to see you at the trade show last week. We much enjoyed the dinner with you and your wife and sincerely hope that you had a safe and pleasant trip home.

As to the proposed cooperation with Gaertner, I have discussed the idea with Gaertner's management. I am pleased to say that your proposal has been met with enthusiasm, and I have taken the liberty of drafting a preliminary written agreement, which I am attaching. May I ask you to read this and let me have your comments at your earliest convenience?

I certainly hope that we will have an opportunity to welcome you in Germany some time in the near future. We would be honored to be able to show you not only our factory but also the sights in our beautiful city.

My best regards to your wife and to Mr Xu and Mr Li.
Ms Gao also sends her very best wishes.

With kind regards
Thomas Baker

Dear Mr. Baker

Thank you again for the pleasant meeting at the recent Home Living Trade Fair. I trust you had a good trip back to Germany and have been able to catch up with your work.

Further to our conversation on Friday, I would like to confirm my interest in a licensing arrangement for Gaertner espresso machines. As far as our present cooperation with Couleur Café is concerned, it now appears that the company is due to be taken over by Gastex and that we will be released from the contract in the near future. This places us in a new situation and confirms our interest in your company. As I was saying at the show, we would be interested in obtaining exclusive rights for the Italian market. Conditions with respect to advance payments would still have to be negotiated, but I am confident that we will be able to come to an agreement.

I am eager to hear your views on this matter.
With best wishes
Gianna Bertani

Owner and Managing Director
Squisito

2 **Read the three emails again and find more formal ways of expressing the following phrases. Write corresponding phrases next to the ones below.**

Say hello to …	My best regards to …	
		Please let me know what you think …
I could arrange another appointment …		
		… as soon as possible …
We still have to talk about the terms …		
		It was nice to …
I went ahead and wrote up …		
		They thought your suggestions were good …

3 Look at the emails in exercise 1 and find expressions which refer to something previously discussed.

A As I mentioned in …

Expressions of reference

4 Use the expressions of reference you have listed above to complete the gaps in the following sentences.

1 .... at the show, we would be willing to talk about a discount for bulk orders.

2 .... our discussion last week, I am pleased to say we will be able to offer the discount you requested.

3 .... the long delivery period is concerned, I think we will be able to find a solution to the problem.

4 .... our new product, I regret to say that its launch has been delayed.

5 The lead requested information .... our environmental and safety standards.

6 You will see that I have provided for a 5 % discount ....

5 Unscramble the following to make correct sentences. Then use the sentences to create an email to a trade show contact.

1 a very wide range | I was saying | only one model | at the show | as | this is | in

2 at the number below | our representatives | an appointment | you would like | with | please call Samantha Evans | one of, | just in case | to arrange

3 catalogue | price list | I am taking | attaching | and | the liberty of | our latest

4 in Frankfurt | visiting our exhibit | thanks very much | for | the recent show | at

5 meets your needs | I am | to find one | that | confident | you will be able | that

6 we are | it was | our state-of-the-art food processor | to demonstrate | of which | to be able | especially proud | a pleasure

6 Find the words and phrases in the email that create an especially warm and friendly tone.

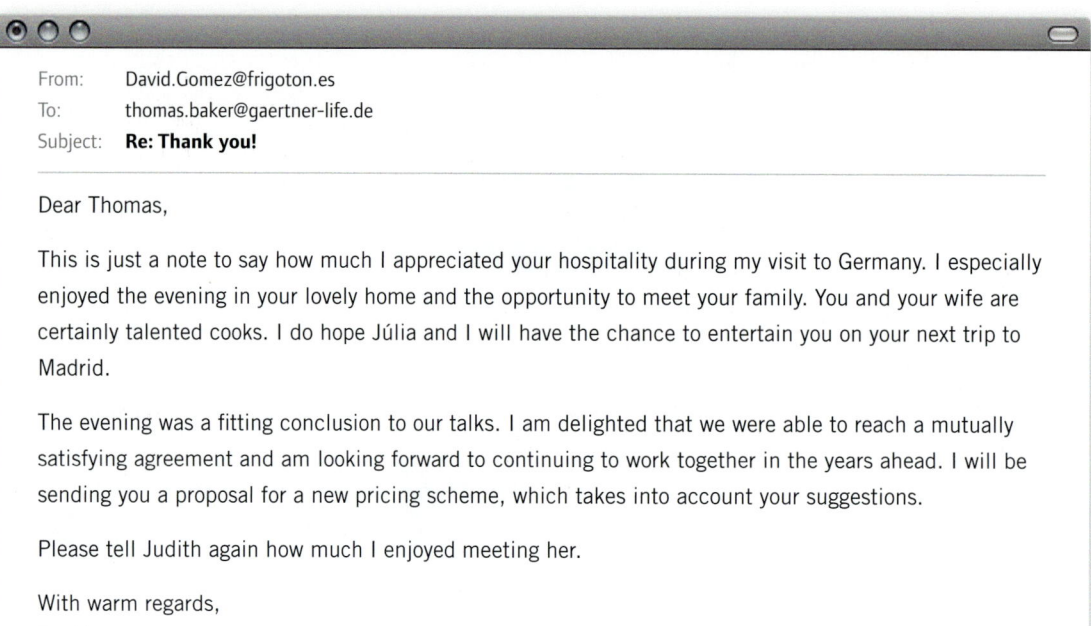

From: David.Gomez@frigoton.es
To: thomas.baker@gaertner-life.de
Subject: **Re: Thank you!**

Dear Thomas,

This is just a note to say how much I appreciated your hospitality during my visit to Germany. I especially enjoyed the evening in your lovely home and the opportunity to meet your family. You and your wife are certainly talented cooks. I do hope Júlia and I will have the chance to entertain you on your next trip to Madrid.

The evening was a fitting conclusion to our talks. I am delighted that we were able to reach a mutually satisfying agreement and am looking forward to continuing to work together in the years ahead. I will be sending you a proposal for a new pricing scheme, which takes into account your suggestions.

Please tell Judith again how much I enjoyed meeting her.

With warm regards,
David

Can you find additional examples from exercise 1, email B?

7 Now match the sentence parts below to create sentences that are warm in tone.

1 This is just a note to say how much I	appreciated	talk to you again last week.
2 I especially/really/certainly	be honored	the opportunity to get to know your family.
3 It was a great pleasure	enjoyed	the sightseeing tour of your interesting city.
4 I sincerely	hope that	to have the opportunity to entertain you
5 We would	to be able to	during your next visit.
		you had a pleasant return journey.

8 Heard in German C-Suites. How do you feel about the following quotes from German managers?

If you ask me, all of these polite expressions are just a little over the top. The people I send my emails to have to accept that Germans are just not like that.

Why all this fuss about making an email sound friendly? The main thing is to get my message across.

I don't have time for all these niceties. That's what I pay my secretary for.

9 Use the information in the following lead form to write an email to a new contact.

Gärtner Life GmbH – Lead Form
Household Appliances and Cookware

Trade Show:	Home Living
Rep Name:	Melissa Oliver
Rating of prospect (1–10):	6
Contact Name:	Adam Mitchell
Company Name:	Creative Kitchen Ltd.
Company Details:	Creative Kitchen, 83 Market Street, York YO1 83U, Adam.Mitchell@CreativeKitchen.co.uk
Company Profile:	Importer of high quality kitchen appliances; high-street chain
Product Interest:	Induction cookware; food processors
Buying Time Frame:	Not specified
Comments about Prospect:	Expressed interest in above products. Catalogues not available at time of visit. Indicated he might be interested in visit from rep.

10 ◁27 Melissa Oliver, Gärtner agent for the U.K., calls a new contact, Jagdeep Sharma, purchasing manager for a chain of British department stores. Listen and answer the questions below.

1 Why has Melissa called Jagdeep?
2 Why does Jagdeep say he hasn't contacted Melissa?
3 Under what conditions would Jagdeep be interested in a demonstration?

11 When approaching new customers it is important not to offend them by asking questions that are too direct. How would Melissa rephrase the very direct phrases on the left? Listen to track 27 again if want to double-check.

Direct

More subtle

1 Did you get the catalogue?

I just wanted to check that you received our catalogue.

2 I know you're interested in …

3 Have you considered our offer?

4 I'll just bring the machines to your office.

5 When do you want a demonstration?

12 Look at your file cards and carry out a follow-up telephone call. Before acting out the call, decide on an industry and a specific product together.

▷ Partner A, p. 59
▷ Partner B, p. 61

13 Evaluating a show. Read the postings on the internet forum www.evaluate.com/node/391. Which criteria do the speakers employ to evaluate the trade shows? Complete the mindmap below.

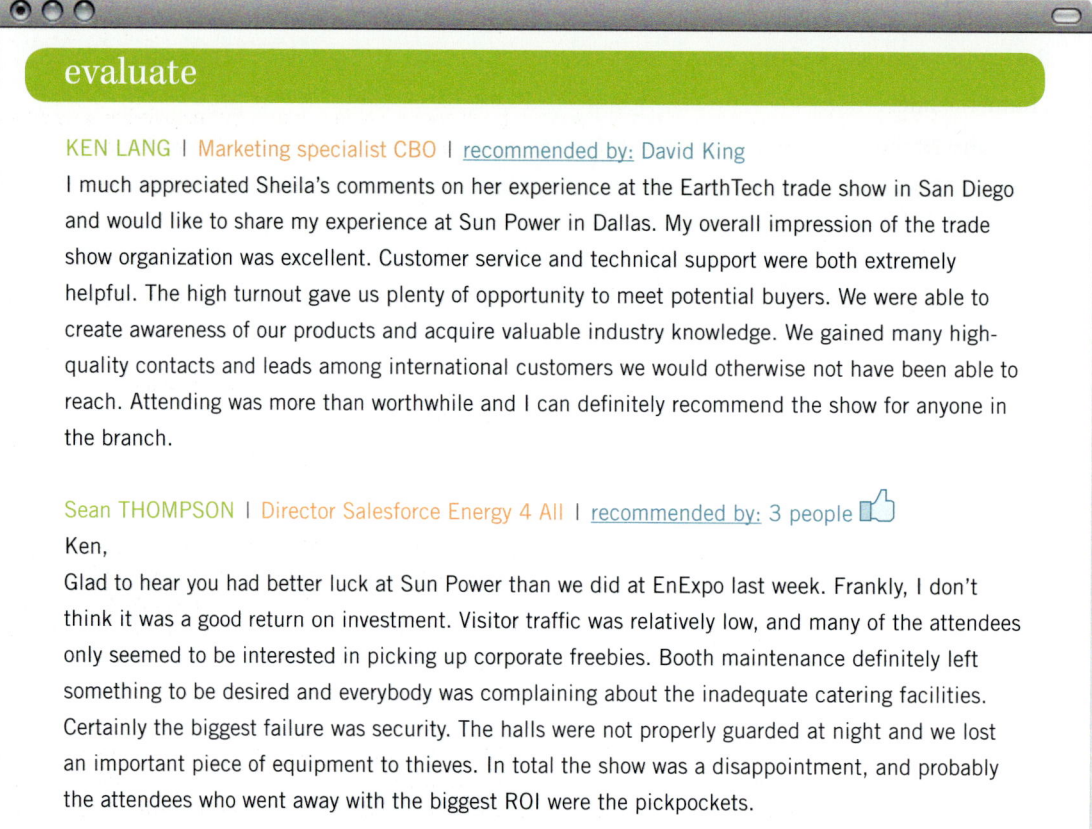

evaluate

KEN LANG | Marketing specialist CBO | recommended by: David King

I much appreciated Sheila's comments on her experience at the EarthTech trade show in San Diego and would like to share my experience at Sun Power in Dallas. My overall impression of the trade show organization was excellent. Customer service and technical support were both extremely helpful. The high turnout gave us plenty of opportunity to meet potential buyers. We were able to create awareness of our products and acquire valuable industry knowledge. We gained many high-quality contacts and leads among international customers we would otherwise not have been able to reach. Attending was more than worthwhile and I can definitely recommend the show for anyone in the branch.

Sean THOMPSON | Director Salesforce Energy 4 All | recommended by: 3 people

Ken,

Glad to hear you had better luck at Sun Power than we did at EnExpo last week. Frankly, I don't think it was a good return on investment. Visitor traffic was relatively low, and many of the attendees only seemed to be interested in picking up corporate freebies. Booth maintenance definitely left something to be desired and everybody was complaining about the inadequate catering facilities. Certainly the biggest failure was security. The halls were not properly guarded at night and we lost an important piece of equipment to thieves. In total the show was a disappointment, and probably the attendees who went away with the biggest ROI were the pickpockets.

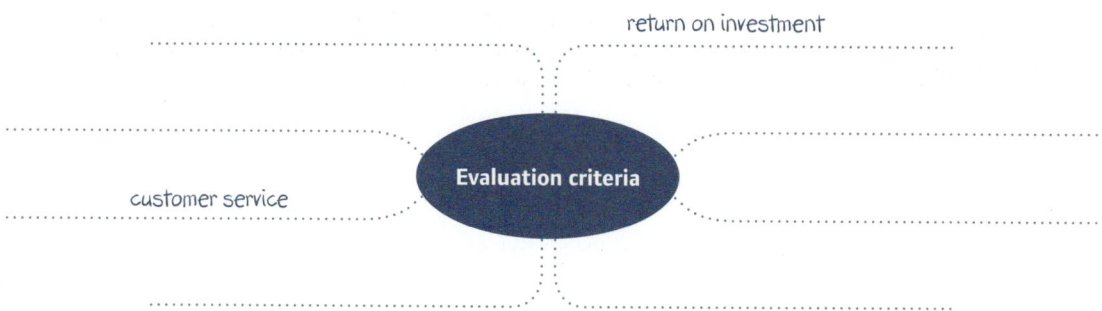

return on investment

Evaluation criteria

customer service

How would you rate your last trade fair experience?

LINK

The Show must go on!?

Follow Mike

Are trade fairs a remnant of the past? I don't think so. Real-life trade fairs will never be replaced by other forms of marketing communication. You can twitter and tweet before and after, but the real benefit of meeting up with customers, discussing conditions face-to-face with suppliers, getting feedback from partners, and observing the competition – is that it's live.

12 days ago • Like

Follow Latifah

Latifah C. With more and more attendees employing new technologies and new forms of marketing, trade fairs will become even more competitive in the future.

11 days ago • Like

Follow Victoria

Victoria Allison Costs for the Frankfurt Book Fair have rocketed this year. For the money we will spend on attending the fair we could easily do weekend workshops for all our customers in luxury venues. However, we simply cannot afford not to go to Frankfurt and we cannot afford to look small-time, either, as people would immediately start making assumptions and question how well the company is really doing.

9 days ago • Like

Follow Rebecca

Rebecca Waters I don't know, Victoria. We've completely stopped attending trade shows as an exhibitor. You're trying to show off your products in an extremely noisy environment – and in the presence of all your competitors. People's attention span is very short and they are bombarded with other pitches and forget 80 percent of what you told them. Is it really worth it?

5 days ago • Like

Follow Devin

Devin Hughes It may be true that trade show attendance is down as companies try to save money, but this means that the attendees who were just out for a free vacation in the first place have been filtered out and that the ones remaining are seriously looking for business partners.

3 days ago • Like

Follow Max

Max D. Gone are the days when even students would rent out their cupboard under the stairs for 500 bucks per night and whole cities became just one big trade show. These large megashows are being replaced by more intimate gatherings such as B2B marketing events and in-house exhibitions.

2 days ago • Like

Over to you

Which of the statements do you agree with?

What are other trends you've become aware of?

Take part in the discussion and write your own prediction for the future of trade shows.

Background

The British retailer Premium Furniture Ltd has registered for the annual Italian Furniture Show in Milan and has booked a large stand (40 m²) to display all their major new developments. Many of the company's best suppliers are Italian. The show is an excellent opportunity to meet them as well as others of the approximately 60,000 furniture manufacturers operating in the country. Italy is an important market for the growing company. Flights have been booked and the Logistics Department has arranged for the exhibit to be shipped. One week before the show the Sales Manager finds a rather dramatic message from the trade show organizer … 28

A little later, an email arrives …

> Due to circumstances beyond our control, Halls D, E and F are temporarily unusable. For exhibition participants who had reserved booths in these buildings, Event Management Milan has booked an annex located about 2 km from the conference center. Since capacity is limited, booth space at the new location is restricted to 10m². Municipal bus transportation is available between the sites. Please confirm these new arrangements as soon as possible.

Assignment

1 Put yourself in the position of Premium Furniture Ltd. One of you is the Sales Manager, the other, Vice President for Sales and Marketing. Work out a strategy for dealing with the new situation.

Sales Manager

As the sales manager in charge of the show, you need to talk to the Vice President for Sales and Marketing, and explain the problem. Explain why trade show attendance is so important. Prepare a few arguments that will convince the VP to give the go-ahead for the show, e.g.

· Many of your most important suppliers will be attending the fair.

Vice President for Sales and Marketing

As the Vice President for Sales and Marketing, you have to approve trade fair participation, which is already stretching Premium's budget. The company can't afford to waste money on a show which could fail.

Think about conditions that need to be fulfilled so you can give your approval, e.g.

· Transport to the annex must be guaranteed, e.g. by an exhibition shuttle service

2 After you have agreed on a new strategy get in touch with the event organizers and customers.

Sales Manager

Write an email to the conference organizer informing them of your new needs, e.g.

· The annex must provide IT facilities.

Vice President for Sales and Marketing

Write to your business partners and convince them that it will be worth their effort to visit your display in spite of the inconvenience, e.g.

· There will be a regular shuttle service from the main exhibition center to the annex.

Share your email with a partner, asking him / her if any changes are necessary.

Background

Your company has received an invitation to a networking event leading up to the most important upcoming trade fair of your industry.

From: Best Practice Network
Subject: Best Practice Networking Event at the P&W Trade Fair

Best Practice Networking Invitation

We would be delighted to welcome you at this year's BPN event at the Summerville Event Center on 13 June. This matinee will give you the unique opportunity to share your experience with leading Best Practice experts and peers from your industry in order to make your trade fair presence a lasting success. Keynote speaker Susan Freytag is going to tell us about award winning stand designs, which can lead to tremendous success at trade fairs.

During a "talk & share" session from 11 a.m. to 1.30 p.m. we would like to make best use of your expertise. Why don't you join us in a series of five minute Best Practice presentations and share your insights with your peers?

Volunteer speakers are asked to register below by the end of the month.

We look forward to seeing you at the Summerville Event Center for what promises to be a very exciting and productive event.

Benjamin Deagan
BPN Event Management

[Register]

Assignment

1. Write an email inviting a close business partner of yours to join you in the event.

2. Your team leader has asked you to volunteer as speakers at the BPN event. Practice your presentation together. Include the following points:
   - why your company attends trade fairs
   - how you prepare for trade fairs
   - what you do to create a welcoming stand atmosphere
   - how you attract visitors to the stand

3. ◁)29 Your presentation at the BPN event was a great success. You've been asked to serve as a consultant to help improve the presentation held by a young start-up company. They have sent you the audio of the last product presentation at their booth. Take notes while listening. What would you change to improve the presentation?

4. Give an improved version of this presentation to the class. Award the best presentation.

Background

At the Home Living Trade Fair three weeks ago you met Cesar Ramirez from Mexico and after speaking with him recorded the most important information in the lead form below. At that time a number of points were left open, e. g. exclusivity, royalties and advance payments. Cesar indicated that the two of you would sort out the details in the months to come. Since then you have had no word from him, but as this could be a valuable contact you want to maintain his interest.

Gärtner Life GmbH – Lead Form
Household Appliances and Cookware

Trade Show:	Home Living
Rep Name:	
Rating of prospect (1–10):	9
Contact Name:	Cesar Ramirez (Head of Purchasing)
Company Name:	El Emperador
Company Profile:	chain of up-market department stores located throughout Latin America
Product Interest:	counter-top kitchen appliances, including mixers, blenders and electric ice-crushers
Buying Time Frame:	Mr. Ramirez was very non-committal.
Comments about Prospect:	Expressed interest in above products. Was given our most recent catalogue. Mr. R. said he would keep in touch.
Recorded by:	(Sales Manager)

Assignment

Put yourself in the shoes of a Gärtner sales manager.

1. Ask a colleague to help you write an email reminding Cesar of your conversations. Suggest solutions to the points left open. Make a point of stressing the benefits that working with you could have for his company.

2. ◁30 A number of weeks have passed and you have had no reaction to your email. Then Cesar leaves a message on your voicemail. Listen to the message. This is the worst possible time of year to receive a visitor from abroad. Your appointment calendar is packed for the next month and especially since Cesar seemed to ignore your email, you are tempted to tell him that you have no time to meet. Consult a colleague and decide what the best course of action is. Your boss may want to hear from you, so make a list of points you consider important. Then respond to Cesar's message.

Self Assessment

Congratulations! You have finished English for Trade Fairs and we hope that you have enjoyed learning with this book.

Let's look back at the English goals you had planned on achieving in the needs analysis at the beginning of this book ▷ p. 5. Assess the progress you have made. Be fair to yourself, even if there's always room for improvement.

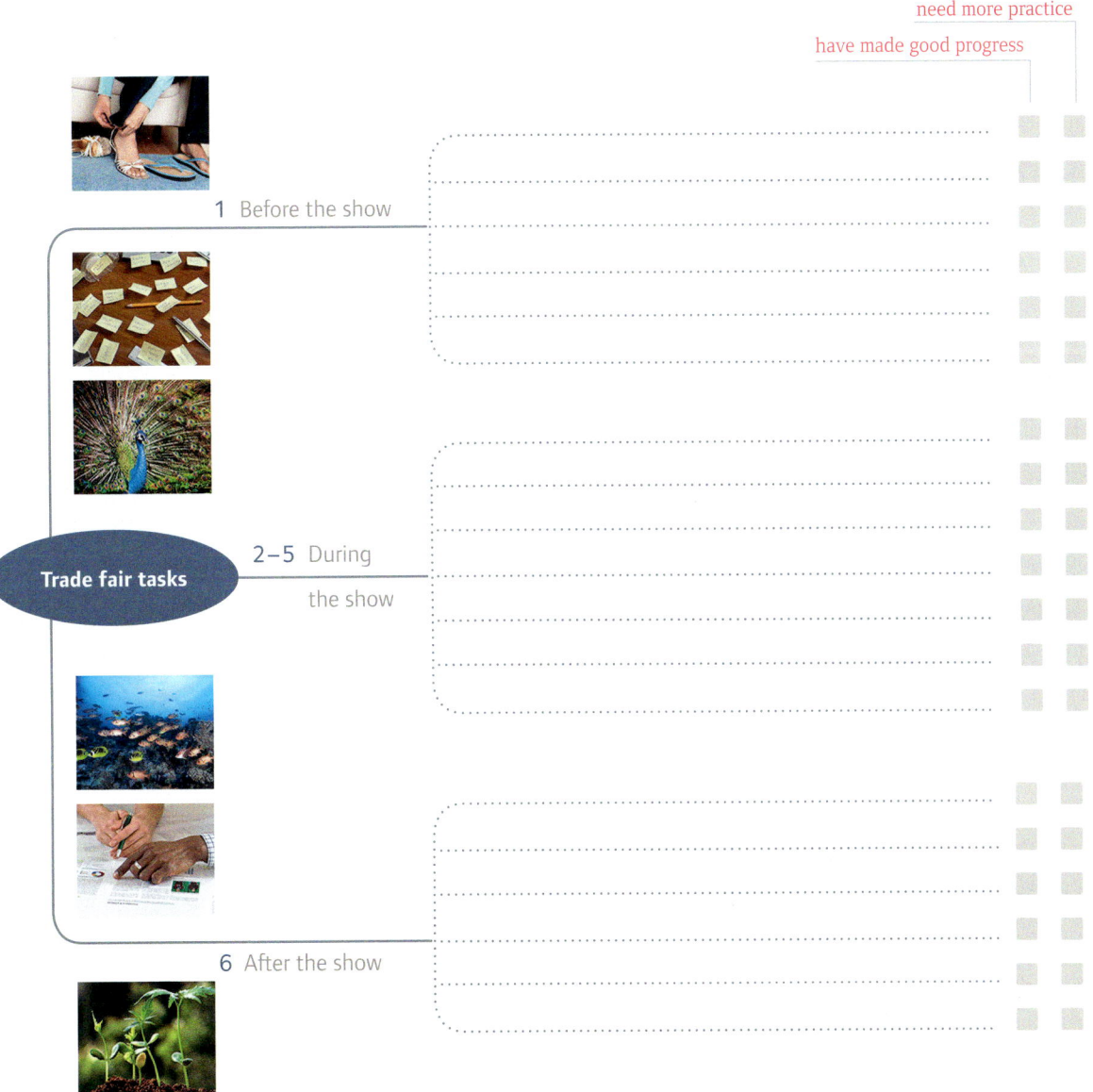

need more practice

have made good progress

1 Before the show

Trade fair tasks

2–5 During
      the show

6 After the show

What are your goals for the future?

Write down three goals that you'd like to achieve over the next three months. Compare your goals with a partner. How are you planning to meet your targets? Do you have any tips and tricks to help each other?

Partner Files

Unit 1   Exercise 5   Partner A   ▷ p. 8

You rented the 45-square-meter corner stand "CS6 Premium" online for your next trade fair attendance. The confirmation you received didn't say anything about the equipment you ordered to come with it. Phone the exhibitor's service and clarify the following points:

- Laminate flooring in beech look?
- High shelves 2.00 meters x 4.50 meters?
- Kitchen equipment? Need two fridges!
- How many sockets? Need at least 8.
- Internet access guaranteed?

Unit 2   Simulation Card   Partner B   ▷ p. 18

Simulation

🖥 Sorting out problems at the stand

Partner B

You are an assistant manager at the exhibitors services. An exhibitor calls with a number of problems. Unfortunately you can't do much until you have spoken to your superior. She is in a meeting in another hall and won't be back for an hour. Express sympathy for the caller's situation and make suggestions for solving the problems. Ask him/her to call back if the problems persist.

Use as many of the phrases listed on page 17 as possible.

Company: ....
....

Problem: ....
....

Time frame: ....
....

Solutions: ....
....

Unit 2   Exercise 13   Partner A   ▷ p. 19

You are the stand manager at your company's booth at this year's trade show. You are very eager to introduce your company's new product and make as many appointments with potential distributors as possible.

Unit 3   Exercise 6   Partner A   ▷ p. 25

Partner B will present his or her company and their services to you. Make sure you receive information concerning the points listed on the right. Ask questions after the presentation if necessary.

- year of foundation
- industry
- main services
- location of headquarters
- number of offices/subsidiaries

▷ p. 42 **Partner A   Exercise 11** **Unit 5**

Complete these prompts. Then try them out on a partner.

I'd appreciate it if you could …   I would be delighted if you …   May I propose that we …
I'm convinced that …   I'm sure you agree …

▷ p. 26 **Partner B   Exercise 9** **Unit 3**

Describe the chart to partner A, who will use your description to complete the template on page 26.

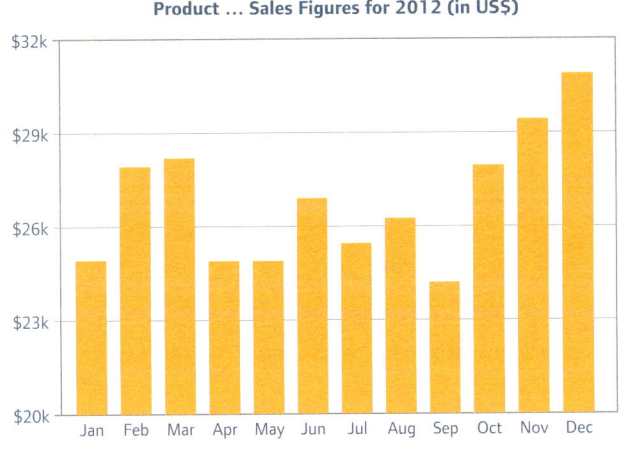

▷ p. 52 **Partner A   Exercise 12** **Unit 6**

A week ago you met a prospective client at a trade show who appeared very interested in your product. You wrote him / her an email and attached a catalogue but have had no reply. Give him / her a call, offering to arrange an appointment. Use your own experience and the phrases you've learned in this unit.

▷ p. 43 **Partner B   Exercise 15** **Unit 5**

You have a meeting with one of your business partners at your stand. You want to discuss what business has been like so far and the potential volume of business within in the next twelve months.

Your attitude:

- You have a full day and can't afford any delays. Punctuality and adherence to timelines is very important to you.
- Keep your answers to personal questions to a minimum. You feel that your private life is nobody's business and should therefore not be discussed in a business meeting.
- Ask business-related questions, but behave in a friendly and hospitable manner. Make it clear that you would like to bring business forward, after all business is business.
- You would like to discuss some issues related to your business partner's adherence to deadlines. You prefer giving clear, critical, and target-oriented feedback to show your honesty.
- You would like to end the meeting on a clear decision. You expect your business partners to come up with concrete solutions when problems occur.

Invent a product. Then describe the chart to partner B, who will use your description to complete the template on page 26.

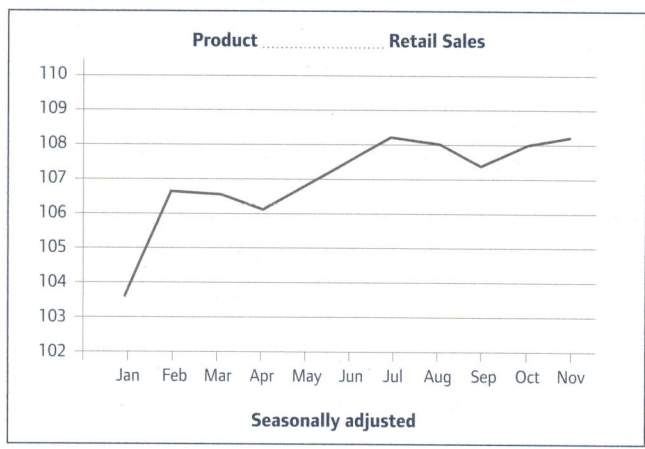

You receive a phone call from an exhibitor who has received a booking confirmation from you. He/she has various questions concerning the CS6 Premium stand. Use the data sheet below to answer the questions.

CS6 Premium: Corner Stand

Standard equipment:

High shelves: 2 x 3.5 meters

Kitchen equipment: 1 fridge, 2nd fridge optional, 12 sockets

Internet access: guaranteed LAN and WLAN

Flooring: laminate flooring in oak or birch look

WIFI   WLAN

Visitor 1: You are a potential distributor and find the exhibited product very interesting and genuinely want to know more about it. However, you are pressed for time and have several appointments today and tomorrow morning.

Partner A will present his or her company and their products to you. Make sure you receive information concerning the following points. Ask questions after the presentation if necessary.

- industry
- main products
- markets
- number of employees
- latest innovation

▷ p. 43 Partner A   Exercise 15   Unit 5

You have a meeting at your main business partner's stand. The target of this meeting is to discuss what business has been like this year and to get an overview of the potential business in the next six months.

Your attitude:

- You arrive 20 minutes late because you had another meeting. Devoting considerable attention to all your business partners is much more important for you than always being on time.
- Ask your business partner a lot of questions about his or her family to express appreciation.
- It's very important for you to have a very positive relationship with your business partner. Use a lot of supportive phrases such as *I see / Sure* or *Absolutely*.
- Your business partner wants to discuss open issues with you related to your adherence to deadlines. Avoid giving open or critical feedback. Be evasive and try to get around using the word *no* or other negative expressions. A harmonious relationship is more important to you than open criticism.
- When your business partner wants you take a decision, try to get around it. You need to talk to your boss first and following the hierarchy in your team is very important to you. Taking decisions without your boss' consent would seem disrespectful and like a breach of trust to you.

▷ p. 42 Partner B   Exercise 11   Unit 5

Complete these prompts. Then try them out on a partner.

Could you imagine …?   It's been a real pleasure …   I'd like to suggest …
I hope you have had a …   It's been a real pleasure ….

▷ p. 43 Exercise 15   Unit 5

You observe a meeting between two different business partners who have very different attitudes. Take notes answering the following questions.

1 How did the meeting go?
2 Were there any major impediments to the communication process?

3 Did it end on a positive note?
4 Is there any advice you could give them for the future?

▷ p. 52 Partner B   Exercise 11   Unit 6

A week ago you attended a trade show and visited a stand with a very interesting product. You gave the booth manager your card and asked for a catalogue to be sent to you. Since the show, things have been so hectic that you have completely forgotten about it. You are still interested but are under a lot of time pressure at the moment. Make an arrangement that suits your needs.

▷ p. 19 Partner C   Exercise 13   Unit 2

Visitor 2: You have time to kill and don't really care about the product. You would like to chat with the stand manager, have a good time and collect a couple of freebies.

Unit 1 — Warm-Up 🔊 02

■ *Sue Grayson* ● *Markus Hildebrandt* at a trade fair seminar

■ Coffee for you too?

● Oh, yes please. Thank you.

■ You're welcome. So, as I was saying … My company has more or less decided to reduce trade fair attendance. I mean just look at the cost of stand rental, services, security …

● Don't forget accommodation and travel expenses!

■ Right! Last time we were at the CONVEYTECH in Hanover, our usual trade fair hotel had increased its prices again by at least 15 per cent.

● Oh, yes, next time we'll have to bring our own tents … Not to mention the food!

■ I know what you mean. We always order an extra fridge for the stand, so that we can store our own stuff there.

● Yes absolutely, there are always a lot of costs involved. But then, you know, we won at least two major new customers at the last trade fair. So, I don't know …

■ You did? That's fantastic!

● Yes, our sales manager is really very good at networking. He definitely takes an opportunity when he sees it. So, for us the trade fair did pay off.

■ Yes, I think you might have a point there. We also invite all our important customers to the fair. And then, it's always interesting to see what our competitors are up to.

● Absolutely! Look, it's ten past. Shall we go in again? So, what was the topic of the next workshop?

■ Optimizing trade fair-related ROI. Seems like something we're both interested in, isn't it?

Unit 1 — Exercise 2 🔊 03

► *Danil Antonov*, CTMove ● *Diana*, NTFC

► NTFC, exhibitors service. Diana speaking. How may I help you?

● Hello. This is Danil Antonov from CTMove. I'm calling from Germany.

► Hello. Sorry, may I have your name again, sir?

● Yes, sure. My name is Danil Antonov and I'm calling on behalf of CTMove. I have been trying to fill in your online order form to book a stand for the CONVEYTECH in August. But I'm afraid there are a couple of things I need your help with.

► Certainly. What exactly do you need to know?

● Our company would like to book a corner stand of about 30 square meters. Unfortunately, I haven't been able to find the price per square meter anywhere on the form.

► Well, in that case you will probably have to look at our booth packages. There you can book your stand with a fixed stand configuration.

● Oh, I see. The booth I would like to have is called Technical Premium. Does that come as a booth package?

► Yes, it does. The stand size is 35 square meters, it's 3 meters tall and it is bookable at a rate of 2,545 pounds, that would be, let me see, about 3,000 euros.

● I see. Now, what about your electricity and water costs?

► Electricity, water and compressed-air are all included in the stand rental if you book it as a booth package. The stand also comes with velour carpeting, one spotlight per five m² stand size, a cross beam system, and preliminary as well as daily cleaning.

● Great. We were also thinking of ordering some rental furniture, like high tables and shelves for example.

► Yes, those are an extra booking, mind you. Actually, our website leads you directly to the rental furniture services. Just click on "booth package" and you will be offered a wide range of chairs, high tables, counters, racks, shelves, displays etc.

● Excellent. Now, just one last question … Do you offer any security services?

► Certainly. Surveillance cameras are in operation in all halls 24/7. You also have the option of booking a security guard for your stand. Would you like me to email you the link?

● Yes, please. That would be great.

► No problem. Is there anything else I can help you with?

● Oh yes. I almost forgot … could you also email me some information on how we can transfer and load our equipment into the hall? Are there any forklifts available? And our fitters would also need to know the setting-up times.

► Of course. The halls are open for loading and unloading from 6 am to 11 pm. I'll send you a ground plan. May I have your email address?

● Yes, certainly. It's Danil.Antonov@CTMove.com

► OK, let me read that back to you: Danil.Antonov@CTMove.com

● That's correct. Thank you very much. You've really been very helpful.

► Pleasure, Mr Antonov. Hope to see you in Birmingham then. Good-bye.

● Thank you. Goodbye.

Unit 1 — Exercise 10 🔊 04

◆ *Arvid*, Vervox ► *Danil Antonov's* answering machine

◆ You have reached CTMove. This is Danil Antonov's office. Unfortunately, I am unable to personally answer your call at the moment. Please leave a message after the beep and I will call you back as soon as possible. Thank you.

► Hello Mr Antonov, this is Arvid Petersson from Vervox. I'm calling about the CONVEYTECH trade fair. I'm going to be at the fair from August the 10th to the 12th. Could you arrange an appointment with Bernard Fletcher for me, preferably on the tenth of August at around 3 pm? Also, I would appreciate it if you could send me three complimentary tickets, or maybe even four, if possible. Thanks in advance. Oh, and if you have any questions you can reach me on my cell phone at 0046-707 987 896. Thanks. Bye.

Unit 1 — Exercise 13 🔊 05

► *Danil* ■ *Kelly*

► Kelly, can you hand me the checklist? Thank you. Great. Let's see.

■ We've decided for the booth package, haven't we?

► Yes, that's right. The Technical Premium stand.

■ Premium sounds good. Does it have a bar and a fridge?

► Well, I don't know about the bar, but we've ordered a fridge. Let's check what we need to take along. We're going to use the displays from the last trade fair, so we need scotch tape, push pins, …

■ What about the Velcro strips for the decoration fabric?

- ▶ Right. Hadn't thought of that. Good. What else, gaffer tape, rubbish bags and towels …
- ■ The stand will be set up for us, right?
- ▶ Yes, FairBuild will see to that, and our fitters will help us with the racks and the literature stands after they have set up the HG7 in the show room. And Peter from IT will see to the computer equipment and make sure we've got internet access. Oh, that reminds me, some additional extension cables and an adaptor and we need the USB sticks with our company logo …
- ■ And what about a spare screw driver kit and a hammer?
- ▶ Good idea. The fitters should see to that. Have the clipboards with our logo been delivered yet?
- ■ Yes, they're in your office.
- ▶ Good, let's make sure we also pack the pens and the paper clips. Kelly, could you make sure all these things go into separate boxes? And please label the boxes, too. I remember the last time I had to borrow gaffer tape from the stand next to ours because ours was hidden under the tea towels …
- ■ Ok, I'll do that. By the way I've also copied the contract, the floor plan and the insurance papers for you. They are on your desk together with 125 new business cards in English.
- ▶ Great. Could you make some spare copies of the documents for Bernard as well, just in case. Oh, and don't forget the duty roster. Great. So far so good … Now let's talk about the folder with the trade fair forms. Have you been able to complete that?
- ■ Well, I've found the visitor record forms and the contact forms. But somehow the English and German report forms got lost. I've only been able to come up with the Spanish version …
- ▶ Hm, I'll see to that.

2nd part track 13

- ■ Speaking of forms, what do we need those lead cards for? Bernard said we should collect as many business cards as possible. Won't we find all the necessary info there?
- ▶ Well, business cards don't tell you which contact might turn into a hot lead. And they don't reveal anything about the visitor's special interests. At the end of a trade fair day it can even be difficult to remember what industry they were in.
- ■ Right. So, we use the lead cards during discussions?
- ▶ Exactly. Once you enter into a serious discussion with a potential new customer you jot everything down on the lead card. Industry, business area, needs, further contacts, anything that might be of interest to us … This will then be consolidated in the report form which goes to sales.
- ■ Oh, I see. That's Christiane's job, isn't it?
- ▶ Right. She's our lead manager and is responsible for the follow-up activities.
- ■ And what's a post-show evaluation sheet?
- ▶ Shall we talk about this post-show?
- ■ Ah, OK, sure no problem. I've also printed out all the contact details of the fair organizers, you know, the utilities, the security people and so on.
- ▶ Excellent. What would I do without you, Kelly?
- ■ Well, you'd go to the fair without any business cards like last time.
- ▶ Oh! Don't remind me of that.

Unit 1	Exercise 14	◊ 06

See 2nd part track 13

Unit 2	Exercise 7 Dialogue 1	◊ 07

- ● *Exhibition Services* ◆ *Marge Wilson,* Bodybild

- ● Good morning. This is Exhibition Services. How can I help you?
- ◆ Good morning. This is Marge Wilson. I'm calling from hall 1, booth 47.

- ● Hall 1, booth 47. And your company name, please?
- ◆ The name of the company is Bodybild. I'm calling because I'm very concerned about the state of our stand. We were assured that the stand would be cleaned every evening. Evidently the cleaners weren't here last night. The rubbish should have been removed, but it wasn't and the carpet is filthy.
- ● I'm sorry to hear that. The cleaning service should have cleaned your booth last night.
- ◆ Well, something must have gone wrong, because there's dirt everywhere. This is completely unacceptable. We need to have a presentable space by the time the doors open, and that's in half an hour.
- ● We'll send somebody over.
- ◆ Well, would you mind doing that immediately? We have important clients coming and can't afford …

Dialogue 2

- ▶ *Sergei Smirnov,* Icesports ■ *Andrew,* Exhibitor Services

- ▶ Hello. Yes. This is Sergei Smirnov at IceSports. I need to report a theft. We're missing a laptop and a portable printer from our booth. I can't believe it. It was there just a few minutes ago and we were barely gone and …
- ■ Sorry, could you slow down please? If I understand you properly, a laptop is missing.
- ▶ Not only a laptop but also a portable printer.
- ■ Let me take down the details on this. What's your stand number and how did it happen?
- ▶ Well, I had just run over to the snack bar for a cup of coffee. There was a security guard just a few yards away, but when I came back, the laptop and printer had disappeared.
- ■ So, the equipment hadn't been secured to the stand structure?
- ▶ I'm afraid, I was just out for a quick coffee …
- ■ Well, you know, the equipment ought to have been secured and any unsecured equipment shouldn't have been left unattended. Is there any means of identifying the equipment – I mean can you give us the makes and serial numbers?
- ▶ Well, the laptop was a, er, a Dell, I think, and the printer was a, – Hey Vadim, what kind of a printer was it? – Hello. Can you hear me?
- ■ Yes.
- ▶ The printer was a 3 DL.
- ■ I'm sorry, we need the brand, the serial numbers and any distinctive features; otherwise it's impossible to identify your equipment should it be found.
- ▶ I'm afraid I don't have that information at the moment. I'll have to contact headquarters.
- ■ Well, as soon as I have the details, I'll submit the report to the police and hope for the best. I'd like to recommend a security locker for the night. No one has ever been able to break into one of those …

Dialogue 3

- ◆ *Francoise*

- ◆ Well, for one thing, the space simply doesn't have enough power outlets.
  Yes, I know, we did get a map of our space, but it wasn't quite accurate. We've counted three outlets, and we need at least twice that number. And each outlet here has only two sockets, while we have to have a minimum of four. Yes, of course, we've brought along a couple of extension cords, but we want to use them only in a pinch, as they're really a safety hazard in a small space like this one. Oh – and something else. We ordered four ceiling spotlights and there are only two. We must insist that you move us to a booth with the proper wiring and lighting.

Dialogue 4

▶ *Amrit*, technical support ■ *Joanne Stewart*

▶ Technical support. This is Amrit speaking. How can I help you?
■ Hello, this is Joanne Stewart in Hall A, Aisle 3, Booth 27. We're having trouble with our wireless Internet connection. It keeps breaking down, and when it does work, the web pages take forever to load.
▶ I'm afraid at the moment I don't have a technician I can send over. In the meantime, I suggest you use a cable to make the connection. All you have to do is plug it into the wall outlet. That should do the job.
■ Unfortunately we haven't brought a cable with us.
▶ Well, if you'll send someone over, I can provide you with a cable, and that will get you hooked up. There should be a technician available by early afternoon.
■ Oh – and something else. We're doing a laptop presentation tomorrow afternoon at 3 and absolutely must start on time. We've ordered a wireless mike and an LCD projector. Could you confirm that order for me?
▶ Just a sec, I'll have a look in the computer. That's right; we've booked the equipment for you. We'll make sure that you get it in time to set it up for your event.
■ Fine. I'll be coming over in five minutes for the cable.

Unit 2 Exercise 11   08

Dialogue 1

◆ *Chris*, Bodybild ■ ● ▶ *3 Visitors*

◆ Good morning. Please come in. Is there anything special I can show you?
■ Not at the moment, thanks. I'm just browsing.
◆ Well, just let me know if you need help.
◆ Come in. Is there anything I can do for you?
● Hi. Just wanted to have a look at your exhibit.
◆ Please do. I'd be happy to answer any questions.
◆ Hi, how are you today?
▶ Fine, thanks.
◆ Just feel free to look around.

Dialogue 2

● *Staffer Paul* ▶ *Brad Zeiger* ■ *Adam Novak*

● Hello. I see you're looking at our new cross-trainer. If you have any questions about it …
■ Well, actually, I was wondering if you distribute to Eastern Europe.
● Just a minute, let me get my colleague, Brad Zeiger. He knows more about that than I do.
▶ Hi! I'm Brad Zeiger. I understand you want to know about our outlets in Eastern Europe. Actually, I have to disappoint you. We're new on the market and don't have distribution channels there yet.
■ Ah, OK, well, my name is Adam Nowak and I represent Connex. We serve as agents for a number of American companies in Poland, the Czech Republic, and Hungary and thought we might be of service to you.
▶ Well, yes, that does sound interesting. When would be a good time for an appointment so you could tell me a little bit more?
■ Just a minute, let me have a look in my diary … Hmm, would tomorrow at ten be convenient?
▶ I'm afraid we're giving a demonstration of our new gym equipment range tomorrow at ten. How about later in the day?
■ I'd be available at four. How's that for you?
▶ I'm sorry, this is going to be a mad house at four. Let's meet in the lobby of our hotel at six. Are you available then?

■ Yes, that's fine. Just give me the details.
▶ OK. It's the …

Dialogue 3

◆ *Katherine* ● *Jordi*

◆ Hi, I see you're interested in our PowerMax FC272 endurance trainer. Is there anything specific you'd like to know?
● Do you think I could use this at home?
◆ Definitely. It's designed for both home and commercial use.
● Mmmm … and what can I do with it exactly?
◆ Well, it lets you do a variety of exercises that cover all major muscle groups and …
● Do you think this would help me lose weight?
◆ Now that obviously depends on how often you exercise. Here, let me give you this brochure. I think you'll find everything you want to know in it …
● I see you also make a massage chair …
◆ I'm sorry you'll have to excuse me. I have another commitment at the moment. Would you mind coming back later?

Dialogue 4

■ *Judith Bell* ● *Staffer Paul* ▶ *Brad Zeiger*, Bodybild

■ Hello. My name is Judith Bell and I'm here to see your colleague Marge Wilson.
● I'm afraid Marge isn't here right now. She has an appointment in one of the meeting rooms and … hey, Brad, when do you think she'll be back?
▶ She's not coming back this afternoon.
● She's not going to be back today. Can I suggest you come back tomorrow?
■ Look, this is the third time I've been here. I didn't make an appointment because Marge assured me that she was going to be at the stand. I'm needed at my own stand and this is taking up valuable time.
● Well, yes, I can sympathize completely.
■ And she hasn't been replying to my voice mail messages. To be perfectly honest, I'm running out of patience.
● I understand the problem. Look, I'll be seeing Marge this evening. Could you give me your cell phone number and I'll ask her to get back to you as soon as possible. I'm confident she wants to catch up with you too.

Dialogue 5

▶ *Brad Zeiger*, Bodybild ◆ *Visitor*

▶ I see you've been looking at our gym equipment.
◆ Well, yes. It's got a lot of interesting features and as a matter of fact, it seems to be very good value for money.
▶ Yes, we like to think so. And I'd like to point out that we offer discounts and free delivery for bulk orders.
◆ Hmm … it could be just what we need. You see, I run a chain of gyms.
▶ Well, then you might be interested in coming to the demonstration of our new range at ten tomorrow.
◆ Thanks. I'll make a note of that. Will that be here at the stand?
▶ Yes, it will. And in the meantime maybe you'd like to have a look at our new catalogue. You'll find the new gym equipment in a special section at the front.
◆ Thanks very much.
▶ Looking forward to seeing you tomorrow!

Unit 2 — Exercise 14 ◁09

▶ *Marge Wilson,* Bodybild ■ *Judith Bell*

▶ Yes, hello, am I speaking to Judith Bell?
■ Yes, this is Judith.
▶ Hi. This is Marge Wilson. We have an appointment at 3:00. I just wanted to say I'm running a bit late. I've completely lost my bearings in this crowd. Maybe you could help me.
■ Sure, which hall are you in?
▶ Well, I think it must be Hall 4. I'm standing at a fountain and at the end of the hall there seems to be an escalator. Hmm, there are rest rooms on my left …
■ Could you give me some sort of landmark, so I can visualize where you are?
▶ Yes, on my right there're huge windows overlooking the bay.
■ Well, then, you're almost there. Just keep going down the hall and take the escalator up to the next level. Go straight ahead until you see the espresso bar on your left, then take a right into – that will be Aisle D. We're in the corner booth at the end of the aisle, just across from the lifts.
▶ Thanks. That helps. I'll be right up.

Unit 3 — Warm-Up ◁10

● *Adriana Bariello* ▶ *Claire Laurent* ◆ *Lan Song*

▶ Oh yes I know what you mean. I think he was only there to get one of our freebies.
● Probably so. Have you seen the new mobile phone covers we hand out for free? They are white with our logo in the middle.
▶ No, I haven't. But I'd like one, too please.
◆ Why did you choose the color white?
● Well, our whole stand is in black and white. I think it looks quite elegant. Why are you asking? What color would you choose?
◆ Well, actually in China white is associated with death or mourning. However, our lucky color is red …
▶ Oh, I see. That's interesting.
● That's really interesting. I'm sure our designers had no idea …
▶ Adriana, how do you usually draw visitors to your stand … apart from the freebies and the good Italian coffee? Any tips and tricks?
● Well, have you ever heard of the "old buddy" strategy?
◆ No, no idea …
▶ Me neither.
● Well, you know people are usually a bit reluctant to speak to people they don't know when entering a trade fair stand. So, to lure them in we place our colleagues Isabella and Frank near the literature rack and the screen where the video presentation is running. They pretend to leaf through the brochures and watch the presentation.
▶ Ah right, I see … and so this way the stand looks well-attended and interesting.
● Exactly. Isabella and Frank "play" potential customers and it's their job to approach the visitors. They usually say something positive about our exhibits or ask for the customer's experience with similar products on the market.
▶ And do they tell customers at some point that they are not visitors but sales people?
● Oh yes, of course. As soon as they find out about the visitor's needs they will reveal themselves.
◆ Hmmm, that sounds interesting. Though I think, this method might not work so well with somebody like me. You know, for many Asian people it is very important to clarify who you are and what your position in the company is before you are able to establish a business relationship. So, this is why we would probably …

● Oh really, so it may look as if they were trying to hide their identities.
◆ Well, …
▶ You know what my American colleague Sue told me? Her boss advised her to walk the aisle and engage as many attendees as possible.
● You mean like walk from stand to stand?
▶ Not exactly. You know how difficult it is to make people enter the stand, especially when they see there's somebody waiting for them inside …
◆ Yes, how do you say … like stepping into the lion's den …
▶ ● Yes, exactly.
▶ So, Sue says they use the space in front of their booth to actively approach attendees and invite them to their stand, handing out freebies, brochures etc.
● Hm, wouldn't that be a bit, well, maybe, pushy or intrusive? I wouldn't really want to do that myself. But maybe one could hire hostesses, crowd gatherers who know how to engage people? Have you ever hired anybody?
◆ Yes, we have. But only to help us at the stand. But Claire, what do staffers from other stands say to that? I've been told some trade fair organizers even forbid exhibitors to place staffers in the aisle …
▶ Yes, that's right. Sue said she once bumped into somebody from the opposite stand approaching the same visitor … Can you fancy that? Quite embarrassing.
● Like fighting over the same prey …

Unit 3 — Exercise 1 ◁11

▶ *Claire Laurent* ■ *Visitor*

▶ Good afternoon. I can see you are looking at our new bluetooth headsets.
■ Well, I, …
▶ Is there anything you are particularly interested in that I can help you with?
■ Actually, I'm looking for new equipment for our call centers in Dresden and Brussels.
▶ Right, well, we actually specialize in system solutions for call centres and I would be more than happy to show you our latest comprehensive range of Bluetooth and VoIP headsets. Maybe I can interest you in our CCS Series?
■ Hm, well, you've got me quite interested, I must say, that sounds really good.
▶ Yes, indeed. May I show you our latest development, the FX Headset? Would you like to have a look at it and maybe just try it on? It really is a state-of-the-art device. The sophisticated microphone provides you with excellent speech intelligibility. The beauty of it is that it is easy-to-handle and just weighs 26 grams, but nevertheless has maximum functionality.
■ Can you tell me something about noise protection?
▶ Certainly. The FX Headset is a very reliable device. It can also be used in extremely noisy environments. With the noise-cancelling microphone, it provides optimal comfort plus clarity. Even in noisy environments, it can filter out background noise. This is a point where we are not willing to compromise. Other highlights of this headset are instant call retrieval and many other capabilities. This system can improve your ability to track and improve agent performance. Like I said, why don't you try it on?
■ Yes, I must say. It feels really comfortable and so light! I could theoretically wear it for hours …
▶ Yes, stylish and comfortable, and believe me, you could wear it for hours!
■ Now, what about prices?
▶ Let me give you our catalogue with the price list. Here you are. This will give you an overview of our terms and conditions.

I'm sure you will find our prices very competitive. Of course, our sales manager, Mr Legrange would be more than happy to discuss a tailor-made solution with you.

■ Thank you. I was actually thinking of a trade fair discount.

▶ Oh, I see. I'm afraid, we only offer trade fair discounts to specialist dealers and resellers. I'm very sorry. But let me tell you what we could do. Why don't I take down your contact details? Mr Legrange could then get in touch with you, and I'm sure we'll be able to find a solution.

| Unit 3 | Exercise 4 | ◁ 12 |

◆ *Lan Song*, NetSpeak ● *Participant*

◆ Thank you very much for being here today. I feel very ashamed for having to do this presentation in English, as I'm afraid my German is by far worse than your English. What I'd like to talk to you about is our future, the future of telecommunications.

● Excuse me, can you speak up a bit or turn up the microphone please?

◆ Oh, yes, certainly … Is that better?
Well, I think we all agree that telecommunications should be made available to everybody everywhere. Now, mobile telecommunications certainly has that option. It is affordable and it is flexible.
Let me talk you through some amazing figures: About 5 billion people around the world already have access to telecommunications, and the numbers are increasing. "The average number of mobile phone subscriptions per 100 inhabitants stood at 122 in the EU-27 in 2008. It has surpassed parity in 23 of the Member States, where there were more subscriptions than inhabitants.
But we from NetSpeak think we can do better than that. Firstly, I'd like to highlight the demographic factor in telecommunications.
As you can see right here, mobile telecommunications can do more than arranging appointments. It can facilitate market processes in remote rural areas, it connects people across closed borders and it is able to enhance learning …

● Excuse me, can I get in here?

◆ Yes sure, fire away.

● Would you mind expanding on the subject of the Indian market?

◆ Well, the Indian telecommunication market has experienced an incredible boom over the last few years with a growth rate of 26 % in 2011 alone, which is partly due to a decrease in landlines and to an increase of disposable income.

● I'm sorry. I didn't quite catch that.

◆ Oh, I'm sorry. What I was saying was that mobile tele-communications also offers a chance to rural areas in the developing world. We see the world as a whole and we feel responsible for connecting the world. Now, to summarize: Netspeak is able to service these developing markets because we offer high quality products and reliable networks. We develop products that suit customer and market needs! To put it in a nutshell: We enable the world to communicate.
Thank you very much for your attention.

| Unit 4 | Exercise 1 | ◁ 13 |

■ *Workshop Facilitator* ● *Sheila Meyer* ● *Jake Rosen*
▶ *Participant 1* ■ *Participant 2*

■ Welcome to our pre-show workshop on networking. I'm happy to see so many of you here today. Now, I realize that you're all experienced business people, so before we start, I'd like to pick your brains. Now, the other day I was talking to this guy,

who is a bit of a business veteran, and he was saying, "80 % of the leads you get at trade fairs turn out to be useless. So, here's my question to you – why bother coming to Earth Tech for networking purposes when you know you'll be going home with a bunch of business cards and lead forms, most of which you'll be throwing away anyway?

● Hi, My name is Sheila Meyer. Well, I'm sorry but I'm not quite sure I can agree with your business veteran.
For one thing, what about the 20 %? I mean, if I meet 100 people here in just a couple of days and 20 turn out to be my future business partners: suppliers, distributors, maybe people who help us enter a new market, and ten of those turn out to be really reliable long-term business contacts, then that will have a huge impact on our sales. So, I'd be pretty happy with the 20 %. My problem is, you see, my company, we deal with very complex and specialist products. Explaining our products does take quite a while and everybody is always in a rush at the show. So how can I interest people without boring them with technical details?

● I'm Jake Rosen. I can only agree with Sheila. I'd even take it a bit further. My company has just signed a contract with a catering service we met at a trade show three years ago. Now, we didn't need a catering agency back then but now that we do, we remembered their exquisite finger food and here we go! What I'm saying is that at trade shows you have the chance to get a first-hand impression of people. You can meet interesting contacts who you might not be able to include in your immediate business plans. But in the long-term you might be able to do a lot for each other.

■ Well, since teaching networking is my day-to-day business I'm very happy to hear that neither of you wants to see me jobless. And let me assure you, Ms … ?

● Sheila. Please call me Sheila.

■ Sheila, we'll definitely talk about how to be short and sweet even when discussing the most complex products a little later on in the day. But let me ask the others. What are your specific expectations when you say that you're here to network?

▶ Well, I'm looking at this show as an opportunity to establish new cross-industry networks and develop synergies among major decision-makers in waste management.

■ For me it's all about breaking new ground. At the show I want to find out about new market segments that could potentially be interesting for us …

| Unit 4 | Exercise 2 | ◁ 14 |

■ *Workshop facilitator*

■ And here are the topics we're going to cover this morning. Can the people in the back see the screen? Is the mike adjusted loud enough? O.K.
We're going to begin by discussing what networking is and what it isn't. Then we're going to talk about preparing for a networking event. This takes us to the third point, which is personal branding using positioning statements. Our fourth point is building rapport by using good listening and questioning skills. Then we have entrance and exit strategies and as our sixth point follow-up procedures that can help you get the maximum out of a networking event. And, we'll be giving you advice on how to use social media and finally, how to organize your own networking event.
So, let's talk about what networking is not. Let me tell you a story about this business owner who gets an invitation to a networking event …

■ *Doug Katz,* Maestro   ● *Keith Buckley,* Maestro
◆ *Monika Lehmann,* ComPress   ● *Steve Macintyre,* ComPress
▶ *Unknown participant*

■ Do you mind if I join you?
◆ No, please do. Here, I'll just move my bag out of your way.
■ Thanks.
▶ Is anyone sitting here?
■ Actually, I wanted to save this seat for a colleague.
▶ Oh, sorry. I'll look for another.
■ Hmm, choosing the yacht as a venue was really a stroke of genius, wasn't it?
◆ Definitely, and the waterfront is really beautiful at night, isn't it?
■ Sure is! This tops last year's event in Colorado – you know, the networking party at the top of the mountain, when they took us all up in cable cars.
◆ Well, unfortunately I wasn't there myself but I did see it on Facebook. Must have been a fantastic experience. By the way, you were in the networking workshop a couple of days ago, weren't you?
■ Yes, I was, as a matter of fact. Nice to see you again. However, I'm afraid I didn't get your name.
◆ Monika Lehmann, from ComPress, head of marketing. And this is our Sales Manager for the U.S., Steve Macintyre.
● Hi. Pleased to meet you.
■ I'm Douglas Katz. I work for Maestro Removal and Recycling. Oh, here comes my colleague. Monika, Steve, I'd like to introduce Keith Buckley. Keith manages our marketing department.
● My pleasure.
■ So … I see you're from Germany.
◆ Yes, ComPress is based near Stuttgart, but we have a sales operation in the U.S.
● And so what exactly does Maestro do, if I may ask?
■ Maestro specializes in removing and recycling trash, garbage and other waste. Our customers are small to medium-sized municipalities, largely in the West and Southwest. We provide efficient services at competitive rates, thanks to our use of state-of-the-art technologies. In fact, we've been growing at a double-digit rate every year since we went on the market ten years ago.
● Hey, that sounds just like what we learned in the workshop about personal branding. But seriously, it's very impressive!
■ Thanks. We're pretty proud of our success.
◆ Do you happen to have a card?
■ Oh, yes. Here it is. And yourselves?

Last part track 15

◆ OK. Let me give it a try … ComPress is a German company with its headquarters near Stuttgart. We make a wide range of compactor containers – from one-unit models to huge breakaway compactors. We primarily serve restaurants and commercial construction sites. Our compactors are valued for their clean handling and easy maintenance. We're able to offer these features due to a unique patented design … Let me give you our card.
■ Hey, that's a coincidence! We've been looking for an alternative to our present compactors. How about getting together later in the show?
◆ I'd love to. Tomorrow is going to be very busy but the day after should be fine.
■ Great! I'll give you a call on your cell.

■ *Doug Katz,* Maestro   ◆ *Monika Lehmann,* ComPress

See last part track 15

● *Steve Macintyre,* ComPress   ■ *Ravi Gupta,* India Food

● I see you've been watching our video demonstration. Maybe you have some questions I could answer.
■ Very interesting, very interesting. You know, I haven't seen anything like this in my country.
● So where exactly are you from, if I may ask?
■ Sir, I am from India – from the north, to be exact.
● And so you have an interest in compactors?
■ Permit me to give you my card. My name is Ravi Gupta; I represent a chain of food places in Delhi. Every day we do business with thousands of people, maybe tens of thousands. You see, sir, at the end of the day our outlets are filled with paper plates, paper napkins, plastic cups, plastic utensils. This is unsightly, unsanitary. And, you know, Indian society is changing, now women work and every week we have more customers.
● I'm sorry, I didn't quite get that … So – you're in the restaurant business.
■ Yes, sir. We run a chain of restaurants in Delhi, the capital. Our places are very popular; we often have thousands of customers each day. We use disposable cutlery and utensils and at the end of the day we don't know what to do with our rubbish. We also have a lot of kitchen waste.
● If I understand you correctly – you're looking for a solution to your trash problem.
■ Yes, exactly.
● Maybe you could give me some more details, so that we can get an idea of your needs.
■ We have 8 outlets in Delhi – imagine, sir, up to 25,000 customers a day and we are planning to open new outlets next year in Agra, Jaipur and Chandigarh.
● Would you mind repeating that, please? I'm not very familiar with India.
■ The outlets will be in Agra, Jaipur, and Chandigarh. Those places are all in the north.
● Ah, I see. So we're talking about at least 11 outlets with a daily traffic of over 250,000 customers.
■ Yes, yes, exactly.
● Are you saying that so far you haven't been using any kind of compaction system?
■ No, sir, you see, my nephew, whom I've been visiting here, just told me that this kind of technology exists.
● Well, then let's sit down over here in the meeting area and talk about what we could do for you …

● ◆ ▶ ▶ *4 Visitors to the stand*

● You really have an exceptional product. Very state-of-the-art. We ain't got nothing like it it in my country …
◆ Great. So let's meet tomorrow afternoon, how about half four – no, let's make it half five – in that place I was telling you about, you know, the one with the Mexican cooking, what was it called, El Paso, Paradiso …
▶ Oh, hi. I was just browsing. Nice stuff you have here, very unusual design …
▶ We're a very big operation; we have production facilities in Shandong Province – in Zaozhuang, Qingdao, and Zhucheng.

◆ *Monika Lehmann* ● *Visitor* ● *Steve Macintyre*

◆ I see you find our video demonstration interesting.

● Yes, indeed. That's an intriguing product you have.

◆ Yes, our compactors do have some unique features. Are you interested in a particular model?

● No, no, I was just trying to get a general impression of what's new on the market.

◆ And so what line are you in, if I may ask?

● Well, you might say that we're into environmental technology, too.

◆ I see. Well, as you probably know, we produce compactors in a variety of sizes and for a wide range of needs.

◆ And this is your latest catalogue, is that right?

● Yes, it is. Now, what types of material were you interested in processing?

● Well, actually, we use a number of materials …

◆ And what quantities were you thinking of?

● I'm afraid that I can't give you an answer off the top of my head. But maybe you could tell me if you give a discount for large quantities.

◆ I'm afraid I'd have to check with headquarters about that.

● I see.

◆ Well, you know what – maybe you could get exact information about your needs and we could meet for a quick lunch tomorrow.

● I'll have to check my diary and get back to you.
Oh, sorry, it looks like I've got an urgent call. Well, if you don't mind, I'll just take one of these catalogues with me and get back to you later. And if we don't see each other – have a good show!

◆ Speaking of weird attendees, Steve … He didn't even give me his card.

● Monika, if I'm not mistaken, I've seen that guy hanging around our competitor's booth.

◆ You must be kidding …

◆ *Monika Lehmann* ● *Steve Macintyre* ■ *Ravi Gupta*
▶ *Dr. Ashok Gupta* ■ *Waiter*

◆ So are we ready to order?

● Yes, I'll have the superburger. Mr. Gupta, I can recommend them. They're great here – as they say on the menu, 100 % prime grain-fed beef.

■ Oh no … no! My family is vegetarian.

▶ You see, our family is Hindu, and for Hindus the cow is a sacred animal. We do eat dairy products and use leather, but we would never eat beef.

● Oh, I'm terribly sorry. You'll have to excuse my ignorance, Mr. Gupta. You see, I'm not at all familiar with Indian culture.

■ No problem, no problem at all. Many things in the West are new to me too.

◆ Mr. Gupta, what do you think about Mediterranean vegetable couscous? I can recommend that.

■ Fine!

■ Are you ready to place your order?

◆ I'll have the Caesar salad.

● That'll be the classic super burger for me, please – on the sesame roll.

▶ The pizza margherita, for me, please.

■ I would like the Mediterranean vegetable couscous.
And so Mr. Macintyre, what is your position in the company?

● I'm a sales representative for ComPress for the U.S. Strictly speaking, Monika is my boss.

◆ Well, I'm head of the marketing department.

■ Ah, such a young lady for such an important position.

◆ Well, thanks for the compliment but I've actually been with ComPress for the past decade. So … how would that be in India? Is it unusual for women to assume senior positions in management?

■ Oh, we have many women in management positions now. Times are changing.
And did you bring your family with you to San Diego?

◆ Well, Mr. Gupta, you see, I'm not married … and even if I were, my employer would probably not understand if they were travelling with me.

■ Ah, now it is my turn to apologize for my ignorance.

▶ You know, the family is very important in Indian culture, so that's the first thing people often ask about – even in business dealings!

◆ Dr. Gupta, what would we do without you to fill us in on Indian culture?

▶ Well, that's my job …

● And may I ask if you have a large family, Mr. Gupta?

■ Oh, by Indian standards I have a rather small family – one son and one daughter. My son is studying at the Indian Institute of Technology in Mumbai and my daughter is a psychologist. She will get married in October. We have found a very nice boy for her …

◆ Well, I wish them all the best. *(fade out)*
(fade in again) Well, I think it's time to get back to the stand. – Waiter, could we have the bill, please? – Oh, no, Mr. Gupta, Dr. Gupta, lunch is on us.

■ Then I'd like to thank you, Mrs. Lehmann, on behalf of my nephew and myself. It has been a great pleasure meeting you. It was really lucky that I ran into you at the trade show.

◆ Yes, it was a pleasure meeting you. I'll be leaving tonight. But all the best for the rest of the show.

■ Oh yes, and on my way back to India, I'm planning a stop in Germany. I'd like to come to Stuttgart to have a look at your compactors, and then I hope to place an order.

■ *Serge Miller* ● *Inga Bergström* ● *Darius Miller*

■ Yes, quite an interesting article they presented during this last discussion. Though I don't agree with the statement about local companies being preferred to foreign ones in China.

● Well, China is a huge country and I guess one shouldn't generalize, but the article does in a way reflect my experience, really.

■ Oh really? Your company sells cosmetics in shops in Beijing and Hong Kong, right?

● Yes, we do and also in the Shenyang area. I have to admit that my first trip to Shenyang was a disaster. All these forms I filled in beforehand, the talks with the authorities and this legal jungle … I wasn't able to make head or tail of it. It's very different from Hong Kong, where in comparison things ran like clockwork. So, I guess it was a very good idea that headquarters finally decided to work with a local agent on site.

● Have you outsourced your manufacturing site to China or are you looking into China as a new market? You do still have a manufacturing site in Europe, don't you?

● Yes, we do. We have two factories in Poland and France. And we have decided to keep it that way and only sell in China. So, I will be visiting the next industrial fair to explore new distribution channels. How about you, Darius? You're in the furniture industry, aren't you?

● Yes, my company specializes in hotel furniture. We sell to major hotel chains worldwide. At present the fastest-growing market for us is India.

- Do you have a distribution centre in India?
- Yes, we do now. It took me quite some time to find an appropriate warehouse. But we are well-positioned there now. The fitters are a different matter. We often experience difficulties getting them to adhere to deadlines and sometimes also quality problems. My colleague is presently at a cross-cultural training in Bangalore before he launches a training program for our local staff. But as, ehm, what's her name, the lecturer, ehm, Ms Feldman, said, the situation is constantly improving.

Unit 5 Exercise 8 22

■ *Thomas Baker,* Gärtner Life ● *Rita Gao,* Gärtner Life
● *Staffer,* China Ware ▶ *Luan Zhang,* China Ware

- ■ I seem to remember that the China Ware stand is at the end of this aisle.
- ● Right. It's number H78.3. Look, that's their logo over there.
- ■ Ok. Here we are …
- ● Oh and Thomas, don't forget to accept the business cards with both hands. And make sure you read through both sides. OK?
- ■ Yeah, sure. Good morning, my name is Thomas Baker from Gärtner Life. We have an appointment with Luan Zhang.
- ● Certainly, sir. Luan Zhang is expecting you. Let me show you to our meeting area.
- ■● Thank you.
- ▶ Mr Baker, welcome to China Ware. My name is Luan Zhang.
- ■ Luan Zhang. It's a pleasure to finally meet you in person. Let me introduce you to my colleague Rita Gao. She is our branch manager in Indonesia.
- ▶ Mr Baker, Ms Gao, I am honoured to meet you. Let me give you my business card.
- ■ Nice to meet you, here is my card.
- ● It's a pleasure to meet you, too. And this is my business card.
- ▶ Ms Gao, if I may ask, are you from China? You have a bit of a Chinese accent.
- ● Oh, thank you, my mother is Chinese. But Mr Zhang, I have to admit my Chinese is not very good, although my mother tried her very best to keep it alive. But I'm afraid, I haven't been the most eager of students.
- ▶ Your mother must be a very wise person. You shouldn't give up. I'm sure you are a very diligent student.
- ● Well, I try my best but I'm still very much a beginner.
- ■ I must say, this is a very impressive stand, Mr Zhang.
- ▶ Oh no, I'm sure you must be used to something far more adequate and impressive.
- ■ Oh, well … I don't know about that …
- ● Thank you, Mr Zhang. We try to do our best.
- ▶ Mr Baker, Ms Gao, I hope you have had a successful fair day. Would you care to join us for some green tea or coffee?
- ■ No, thank you. Actually, …
- ● That would be lovely! We have enjoyed the fair very much so far.
- ▶ You know we drink a lot of tea in China. There is a proverb that says: Better to be deprived of food for three days, than tea for one.
- ■ Oh really? That's interesting. Actually, I prefer coffee. There's nothing like a strong espresso to keep one's mind awake, right? Well, Mr Zhang, thank you very much again for seeing us today. I'm sure you must be very tied up. As I said in my email, we would like to discuss the benefits that a partnership with Gärtner could offer to China Ware if we did business together.
- ▶ We are all confident that our common efforts will be successful.
- ■ Yes, ehem …
- ● Actually, China Ware has been warmly recommended to us by Stephen Pan.
- ▶ Ah, Stephen Pan, a very honorable man. How did you get to know him?

- ● Mr Baker and I had the pleasure of meeting him during the last Doma Trade Fair in Shanghai. He was most helpful with contacts to the HKETO.
- ▶ Oh, I see.
- ■ Ehem, Mr Zhang, I was wondering if you have already had the opportunity to read through our suggestions on the Zhejiang area?
- ▶ Yes, well …

Unit 5 Exercise 10 ◁23

■ *Thomas Baker* ● *Rita Gao* ▶ *Luan Zhang*

- ▶ I'm sure you're absolutely right there Mr Baker. Do you think you could expand on the range of products you would like to sell with China Ware?
- ■ Yes, I'm positive about this aspect. As you know, Gärtner specializes in high-quality woks, clay pots and steamers. We would be particularly interested in providing the specialist dealers China Ware sells through with our new series of non-stick pans and high-pressure cookers. I understand that there would be territorial restrictions concerning the Zhejiang area.
- ▶ Absolutely. Nevertheless, I'm convinced that China Ware is able to offer you an interesting infrastructure and a well-trained sales force. Shall we have look at the spreadsheet which …
- ● I agree, Mr Zhang, as you probably know, Gärtner also provides excellent after-sales service. Could you imagine broadening the training offered to the sales staff? I'm sure you agree that we would all benefit from a professional after-sales service.
- ▶ Actually, that's an interesting point. We could of course adapt the recruitment of our sales staff to meet these needs. But I'm also sure that our present sales staff are able to deal with all customer enquiries in a satisfactory way.
- ● Oh, I'm sure that goes with out saying. What I actually had in mind were the operational procedures that we could …
- ▶ I'm very pleased about the outcome of this talk. May I propose that we continue our talk after the trade fair?
- ■ Excellent. We would be more than delighted. My assistant will let you have a summary of our results in writing and make a suggestion for another appointment.
- ▶ Oh, thank you. I would appreciate that. Ms Gao, Mr Baker, it has been a real pleasure meeting you.
- ■ Thank you Mr Zhang and we look forward to continuing our business relationship with you and your company. By the way, may I present you with three sets of cooking cutlery utensils for yourself and your team? We have taken the liberty of engraving your and our company logos on it.
- ▶ Thank you very much Mr Baker. I'm sure Mr Xu and Mr Li will feel as honoured as I do by your generosity. Thank you very much. I would be honored if you accepted this small token of our appreciation of your visit. You will find Chinese green tea very healthy.
- ■ Mr Zhang, thank you very much indeed. This is very generous of you.
- ● Luan Zhang, we are the ones to be honored by your taking the time out of your busy schedule to allow us to present our products and company. We look forward to being able to speak to you soon.

■ *Thomas Baker,* Gärtner Life   ▶ *David Gomez,* Frigotón

■ Hello David. It's good to see you again. How are things?

▶ Hello Thomas. Not bad. How are you doing?

■ I'm fine, thank you. How about yourself? How's the family?

▶ Very well, thank you. We are now proud parents of a second baby!

■ That's fantastic. Congratulations! Is it a boy or a girl?

▶ It's a little girl. Her name is Maite. But how's your daughter? Has she started school yet?

■ Yes, she has. And she has started taking Spanish lessons. She absolutely loved it so far.

▶ Wow, I'm impressed. They really start learning languages early these days. She'll be fluent in Spanish and running her own business by the time she turns 18.

■ Well, I don't know. But she is a tough negotiator. So, what do you think, shall we get ourselves a cup of coffee and then move on to business, David?

▶ Good idea, Thomas. Let's do that!

■ So, tell me, how's business at Frigotón?

▶ Well, as you've probably seen, the sales figures for the third quarter look quite good.

■ Yes, right. They look rather impressive, I would say.

▶ Mmmh, yes, but if you look at the regional distribution of sales over the shops you will see that most sales are made in the major towns and cities with more than 25,000 population. Which means, I'm afraid, that sales in the small shops in the rural areas have gone down by 15 %.

■ Oh, I see. That doesn't sound very good. Why do you think that is?

▶ Well, I reckon it's a question of pricing. In the small shops, people feel that in comparison to other competitors we are overpriced. I mean, it's not that people think we don't offer good value for money, but what with the mark up of 7 % last year …

■ Right. I can see your point. So, what do you suggest we should do?

▶ I think we need to adapt to the regional market situation. We have to rethink the pricing, especially in the division of steel pans. What about a promotional price for the new cutlery series?

■ That sounds like a good idea. What if we revised pricing for the first quarter of the coming year and considered a mixed calculation? This way we could increase the …

● *Rita Gao*   ◆ *Ewa Pajak,* Warsaw White Goods

● Hi Ewa. It's great to see you again.

◆ Hello Rita. Thank you. How are you?

● Fine. Thank you. How was the train journey?

◆ Great. Everything went fine.
Rita, would you mind if I began talking shop straight away? I'm afraid, I have a tight schedule today and have another meeting in 45 minutes. I'm really sorry to seem so pressurizing …

● Oh, sure. No problem. One needs to make the most of the short fair time, right? So, you mentioned certain issues with the last advertising campaign …

◆ Yes, that's right. I regret I have to say this, but frankly speaking, we are very unhappy with the way things have been handled from your end.

● Oh, I'm really sorry to hear that. What exactly seems to be the problem?

◆ Well, I'm afraid, there are multiple issues. First of all we didn't get the promotional material on time … you know the

displays for the specialist dealers and the household appliances stores. We actually got them 2 weeks <u>after</u> the Christmas sales had begun. And then the technical data sheets, I definitely remember discussing this with you when …

● Oh, can I get in here, Ewa? I fully understand that this must have been very inconvenient. But concerning the promotional material, I was under the impression that we had agreed on getting this to you well before the Christmas sales. Who have you been in touch with?

◆ Matthias Beyer from Marketing, if I remember correctly.

● Very well. I will certainly sort this out and get back to you as soon as I find out what exactly happened in Marketing. Do you happen to have any figures as to whether this has affected sales?

◆ Thank you. Yes, I do. I've brought them along. I had actually wanted to email them to you on the train. But the connection wasn't very good. So, can I give you my memory stick?

● Great. Thank you. That will be very helpful. Now, you mentioned quite a few issues?

◆ Yes, we've spotted various mistakes in the technical data sheets, especially in the Polish translation. And I'd like to add, not for the first time. Can I suggest you send this to us before giving it to the printers? Somebody from our service hotline could proofread the sheets and make sure everything's correct.

● Excellent, thanks for offering this. I'll see to it and will ask our technical writer to get back to you. Ewa, is there anything I could do to improve the communication between our two headquarters?

◆ Well, it seems to me there are too many people involved. It would be helpful if we could handle things through one point or maybe two points of contact only.

● Right. I see what you mean.
Why don't we arrange another meeting and …

● *Gianna Bertani,* Squisito   ■ *Thomas Baker,* Gärtner Life
■ *Martin Falke,* Gärtner Life

● … Yes, absolutely. I think this is the reason why Starbucks has not been able to enter the Italian market yet.

■ Well, so … Ms Bertani, from what Martin told me I gather you have already discussed various possibilities of cooperation between Squisito and GärtnerLife …

● Well, Mr Falke has already mentioned that you would be interested in entering the Italian market with your new Vivacita.

■ That's right. I have to admit, we are really proud of this espresso machine, and … I would even dare to say it is absolutely able to meet Italian quality standards.

● Well, as you probably know, Mr Baker, we have been a licensee of Couleur Café, the French manufacturer of catering supplies, since 2006. And I have to admit we would be sad to change our co-operation partner.

■ Yes, I know Couleur Café. A very young and innovative company. You know Gärtner is able to look back at 70 years of experience in the manufacturing of coffee makers.

● Yes, I'm well aware of Gärtner's success in the German and Austrian market. Still, if you don't mind me saying so, the Italian market is very special. As I have already explained to Mr Falke, our main target groups are baristas and gourmet coffee shops. We feel that your line of coffee makers would maybe suit other target groups better.

■ I see. Of course the Italian market places special demands on manufacturers in this field. However, we think that with Vivacita we would be able to compete. I mean we are talking about high-quality, long-lasting catering equipment here. Have you seen our latest catalogue? Actually the Vivacita won a design award last year. I strongly feel that …

● That's correct. Well, our contract with Couleur Café is not going to expire before the end of 2015. So, if we decided to give the Vivacita a test-run, would we be talking about exclusive rights here?

■ Absolutely. Gärtner Life would grant the exclusive rights to Squisito at the special conditions discussed before. As to the quantities we were thinking of …

● Hmmm, of course I would have to discuss the royalties with the management.

■ Of course. But as I said, you will find Gärtner Life a very flexible partner.

● Can you also give me an idea of the advance payments you were thinking of?

■ Well, since this would be a special co-operation Gärtner Life would be willing to reduce the advance payment by 50 % for the first year.

● Oh, I see. Aha. Actually, I was thinking of *(fade out)*

■ *(Fade in)* Great! That's good to hear. You mentioned your contract with Couleur Café is going to expire by 2015. Why don't we sit down and sketch out conditions of a possible licensing agreement from then? Mr Falke could send you a first draft before we get down to the nitty-gritty …

● Frankly speaking, Mr Baker, I'd prefer to reconsider your offer. Maybe you could send me a sample of the Vivacita to show to our barista experts?

■ Of course, I'd be delighted to. Are you staying at the fair until Sunday? I could then arrange for a Vivacita to be sent to …

| Unit 6 | Exercise 10 | 27 |

● *Jagdeep Sharma,* Nicholson Ltd.
◆ *Melissa Oliver,* Gärtner Life

● Hello, This is Nicholson Ltd. Jagdeep Sharma speaking.

◆ Hello, Mr. Sharma. My name is Melissa Oliver. I'm calling from Gärtner Life. We specialize in household appliances and cookware.

● Mmh, yes … What can I do for you?

◆ We met two weeks ago at the HomeLiving Trade Show in Frankfurt. You visited our stand at the trade show and left your card.

● Oh yes, that's right.

◆ I just wanted to check that you received our catalogue.

● Yes, yes, I did as a matter of fact. Thanks very much for your email. I'm afraid I've been very busy.

◆ Oh, I know the feeling. If I'm not mistaken, at the show you expressed a special interest in our espresso machines. Since the show we've launched new models that might be of interest to you.

● Ah, yes, of course. I was very impressed by the design and technology – great value for money. Sorry – I just haven't had time to get back to you. You know how it is when you're out of the office for a couple of days – the backlog of work and all.

◆ Yes, of course. I can certainly sympathize. Well, I hope you've had time to consider our offer of arranging a demonstration for you, whenever you can set aside an hour or two.

● Yes, I'd definitely be interested in looking at the various models, providing you have a showroom nearby.

◆ No, we haven't, as a matter of fact, but it would be no trouble to bring the machines to your office. Now when would it be a convenient time for you?

Business Challenge 1

 28

▶ *Luca Mantovi,* Event Management Milano

▶ Yes, hello … this is Luca Mantovi from EMM in Milan. We're the organizers of the upcoming Furniture Show and have your name here as a registered participant. Sorry not to be able to reach you directly. I'm afraid to say … err … that there's been a problem. We've … mmm … had heavy rains and … flash flooding here in Milan and the exhibition hall you were assigned to is under water. Unfortunately, the other halls are full to capacity. But there's no need for concern – we've rented an additional hall where we can provide you with a booth. I'm emailing you the details. Please give me a call if you have any questions. My number is …

Business Challenge 2

 29

▶ *Presenter* ◆ *Participant*

▶ … yes, well thank you for joining me for the presentation of our new … eh … can everybody hear me? … OK, so, the presentation of our new hiking boots – "endurance". The name is "endurance". It took us two years to develop this high-tech shoe, which is very different from all the other shoes on the market.

◆ Can you hold it closer to the camera? I can't see it on the screen.

▶ What is really different is the new flexi-sole. The shoe pairs a Goretex liner and a leather upper, which makes it … eh … almost fully drainable. The wet-grip sole with its special heel locks ensures safe hiking and good traction … even in rough environments, in any terrain actually.
The boot is very light-weight, more like a low-cut walking shoe than one of those heavy, bulky trekking boots you may see presented around here …
If you have any questions so far, please fire away. Now, I'm now going to show you the kind of stress test we carried out to make this one of the most agile and durable shoes ever. As you can see, this is our water tank. Filled with salt water and some gravel and sand at the bottom. In goes the shoe. And this gadget imitates the walking movement with/at a pack load of – uhm – I think 95 kg.
Now, we're going to take this shoe out of the tank in two hours and then we'll see what will have happened. So, if you care to leave your name and email address with Carole there at the entrance of the our booth … and come again in two hours of course then we could check it out together and TrekkingEx will be happy to present you with some of our most popular trekking equipment like our famous sleeping mats and some of these stylish and very practical flasks. Thank you.

Business Challenge 3

 30

● *Cesar Ramirez,* El Emperador

● This is Cesar Ramirez … Well, things have been moving along here faster than I expected. I am leaving for Europe this evening. Your proposal was very interesting and there are some things we must definitely discuss. Can we meet sometime this week? I will be staying at the Excelsior Hotel. You can reach me by email.

Answer Key

Unit 1

Exercise 1
1 visitors 2 smoothly 3 interlinking 4 exhibition grounds
5 trusted 6 venue 7 unrivalled

Exercise 2
1 not mentioned 2 corner stand 3 yes 4 included in stand
rental 5 extra booking required 6 surveillance cameras in
operation 24/7 7 halls open between 6am and 11pm

Exercise 3
Rental furniture and equipment
armchairs, carpet, computer work stations, display cases,
flooring, hooks, literature stands, picture rails, racks, shelves,
stools

Services
additional stand personnel, catering personnel, cleaning
staff, electricity, promotional staff, security services,
visitor management, waste management

Presentation technology
amplifier, audio equipment, data projector, loudspeakers,
plasma screen

Technical equipment
power outlets, sockets, water, high-speed internet access,
lighting

Exercise 4
1 flooring 2 carpets 3 shelves 4 display 5 security
services 6 waste 7 catering personnel 8 promotional staff
9 internet access 10 data projectors

Exercise 7

Model email

Hi Brian,

Thanks for your email about next week's trade fair.

Our flooring can take a maximum load of 5 tons/m², so you
will have no problems with the Convey HG7. You can even
drive in through the gate in Hall 3.

Yes, we have overnight cleaning. Exhibitor services asks
us to ensure that cleaning staff have access to our stand
between 8pm and 2am. Our waste management will provide
containers in hall 3 and 4 for disposing of hazardous
materials such as coolants and lubricants.

Should you have any further questions, please don't hesitate
to get in touch.

Best wishes,
Danil

Exercise 8
1 very pleased to announce 2 as one of our valued
customers 3 be on display for you 4 particularly excited to
be presenting 5 sign up for 6 a leading authority on 7 look
forward to seeing 8 to arrange a personal meeting

Exercise 10
1 The caller's name is **Arvid Petersson**. 2 He wants to
meet **Bernard Fletcher**. 3 He wants to meet on **10 August
around 3pm**. 4 His mobile number is **0046 707 987 896**.
5 He requests **3–4** complimentary tickets.

Exercise 11

Model email

Dear Mr Petersson,

Thank you for your call. Unfortunately, Mr Fletcher is
unavailable on 10 August, however he has suggested an
alternative date: 11 August at 1.30pm. Would this be
suitable for you? Please let me know and I will arrange the
appointment.

Best regards,
Danil Antonov

Exercise 13
Stationery
scotch tape, push pins, Velcro strips, decoration fabric,
gaffer tape, clipboards, pens, paper clips, boxes

Tools
fridge, displays from the last trade fair, rubbish bags, towels,
racks, literature stands, screwdriver kit, hammer

Computer equipment
computer equipment, extension cables, adaptor, USB sticks

Documents
contract, floor plan, insurance papers, business cards, duty
roster, folder with trade fair forms, visitor record forms, contact
forms, English and German report forms, Spanish report forms,
lead cards, post-show evaluation sheet

Unit 2

Exercise 1
Not clean: filthy, messy, soiled, stained, unsanitary
Not working: out of order, broken, clogged, damaged,
jammed, not connected, unusable
Not to be found: missing, gone, unavailable
Not enough: weak, dim, inadequate, poor

Exercise 2
Possible combinations:
carpet: filthy, stained, soiled, damaged, missing, gone
display: messy, broken, unusable, missing, gone
drain: unsanitary, clogged, jammed, not connected, out of
order
exhibit: messy, damaged, unusable, missing, gone
extension cord: damaged, broken, not connected, missing,
gone, unavailable
(fire) extinguisher: out of order, damaged, broken, clogged,
faulty, missing, gone
hooks: damaged, broken, missing, gone
lighting: out of order, dim, inadequate, poor, weak
LCD projector: out of order, damaged, broken, unusable,
missing, gone, unavailable
light bulb: damaged, broken, missing, gone, dim
lock: damaged, broken, jammed, unusable
locker: filthy, messy, damaged, unusable, jammed
mike: out or order, damaged, broken, unusable, not connected,
missing, gone, weak
picture rails: damaged, broken, unusable, jammed, missing,
gone
plug: damaged, broken, unusable, faulty
power (wall) outlet: damaged, broken, unusable,
not connected

rope stanchions: filthy, damaged, broken, unusable, missing, gone
screws: broken, unusable, faulty, missing, gone
skirted table: filthy, soiled, stained, damaged, broken, unusable, is missing, gone
socket: out of order, damaged, broken, unusable, faulty, not connected
spotlight: out of order, damaged, broken, unusable, faulty, dim, poor, weak
WiFi: out of order, unusable, weak, inadequate

Exercise 3
1 damaged 2 stained 3 unsanitary 4 clogged
5 jammed 6 messy 7 unavailable 8 dim

Exercise 4
1 setting up 2 break down 3 come apart 4 tape
5 sockets 6 extension cord 7 put up 8 take it down

Exercise 6
1 plugged (back) in 2 shut down 3 turn off 4 broke into
5 had thrown away / were throwing away / threw away
6 set up 7 take down 8 hang up

Exercise 7
1 **Dialogue 2**: laptop and printer were stolen.
2 **Dialogue 4**: the wireless internet connection isn't working.
3 **Dialogue 1**: booth wasn't cleaned overnight.
4 **Dialogue 3**: booth doesn't have enough power outlets and sockets.

Exercise 8
1 b 2 e 3 g 4 d 5 a 6 c 7 f 8 j 9 h 10 i

Exercise 9
Making a complaint
I'm very concerned about the state of our stand. | We were assured that the stand would be cleaned every evening. | I'm afraid I don't have that information at the moment.

Requesting / Demanding help
Would you mind doing that immediately? | Sorry to bother you, but there's been a misunderstanding about the furniture in our booth. | We must insist that you move us to a booth with the proper wiring and lighting. | We're having trouble with our wireless Internet connection.

Apologizing
I'm afraid I don't have that information.

Offering a solution / Promising help
We'll send somebody over to sort everything out. | I suggest you use a cable to make the connection. | We'll make sure that you get it in time to set it up for your event.

Exercise 10
1 should have noted 2 must have been 3 should never be left 4 ought to have come 5 was supposed to relieve 6 might come by 7 was supposed to have been equipped / was supposed to be equipped 8 should have removed 9 ought to be shipped

Exercise 11
1 c 2 a 3 e 4 d 5 b

Exercise 12
Greeting and welcoming
Please come in. | Let me know if you need help. | Feel free to look around.

Making arrangements
When would be a good time for an appointment? | How about later in the day?

Turning people away
I have another commitment at the moment. | Would you mind coming back later?

Calming people
I can sympathize completely. | I understand the problem.

Highlighting information
I'd like to point out that we offer discounts. | Maybe you'd like to have a look at our new catalogue.

Exercise 14
1 running a bit late 2 lost my bearings 3 I think it must be 4 and there seems to be 5 there are restrooms 6 some sort of landmark 7 where you are 8 overlooking the bay 9 keep going down 10 escalator 11 straight ahead 12 corner booth 13 aisle 14 across from

Unit 3 ....

Exercise 1
1 particularly interested | with 2 beauty of it | just 3 not willing 4 an overview of 5 more than happy to 6 let me tell | take down 7 to find

Exercise 2
1 e 2 h 3 f 4 j 5 c 6 g 7 a 8 i 9 b 10 d

Exercise 4
Phrases mentioned:
I feel ashamed for having to do this in English. | What I'd like to talk to you about … | I think we all agree … | Let me talk you through … | Firstly, I'd like to highlight … | Fire away. | What I was saying was … | To put it in a nutshell, …

Exercise 5
Opening your presentation
I'd like to apologize for my bad German. | I feel ashamed for having to do this in English. | What I'd like to talk to you about is … | What I want to discuss with you is …

Telling the audience about the structure of your presentation
Let me talk you through … | Let me give you an idea of what I will be talking about. | Firstly, I'd like to highlight … | First of all, I'd like to draw your attention to …

Giving new information
I think we all agree … | I believe we can all agree …

Clarifying a point
What I meant was … | What I was saying was …

Summarizing results
To put it in a nutshell, … | What this all boils down to is …

Inviting Questions
Fire away. | Go ahead.

Exercise 7
↑ soaring, surging, rocketing, exceeded, on the rise, gaining in, reaching a peak
↓ experiencing a slump, decrease, decline
→ levelling out, on the same level

Exercise 8
1 gaining in 2 decrease in 3 reached 4 declined to a 5 the same level 6 reached

Exercise 10
1 by 2 in 3 of 4 of 5 At 6 of 7 out of

Exercise 1

He questions the usefulness of trade fairs as a networking tool.

1 brains 2 impact 3 cross-industry, makers 4 ground, segments

Exercise 2

1 Defining networking 3 Personal branding using positioning statements 5 Entrance and exit strategies 6 Follow-up procedures 8 Organizing your own networking event

Exercise 3

1 hosting 2 in conjunction with 3 drawn from 4 Invitees
5 views 6 dedicated to 7 confirm your participation

Exercise 4

1 No, please do. 2 Definitely, and the waterfront is really beautiful at night, isn't it? 3 Yes, I was as a matter of fact.
4 Hi. Pleased to meet you. 5 Oh, yes. Here it is. 6 I'd love to. Tomorrow is going to be very busy but the day after should be fine.

Exercise 5

Name and location of company: (4) ComPress is a German company with its headquarters near Stuttgart.
Type of product: (5) We make a wide range of compactor containers, from one-unit models to huge breakaway compactors.
Target customer: (3) We primarily serve restaurants and commercial construction sites.
Key benefit: (2) Our compactors are valued for their clean handling and easy maintenance.
Reason you can deliver that benefit: (1) We are able to offer these features due to a unique patented design.

Exercise 6

1 We met last year, **didn't we?** 2 You work for Whizz, **don't you?** 3 The booths are well equipped, **aren't they?** 4 We're meeting the new agent this evening, **aren't we?** 5 Ken will be at the stand tomorrow, **won't he?** 6 She works for our major competitor, **doesn't she?** 7 We've arranged to meet this evening, **haven't we?**

Exercise 7

1 I see you've been watching … 2 So where exactly are you from? 3 And so you have an interest in … 4 If I understand you correctly … 5 Maybe you could give me some more details … 6 Would you mind repeating that, please? 7 So, we're talking about …

Opening the conversation

I see you've been watching our video demonstration. |
So where exactly are you from, if I may ask?

Eliciting information

I see you've been watching our video demonstration. | And so you have an interest in compactors? | Maybe you could give me some more details, so that we can get an idea of your needs.

Avoiding misunderstandings

If I understand you correctly – you're looking for a solution to your trash problem. | Would you mind repeating that, please? I'm not very familiar with India. | So we're talking about at least 11 outlets with a daily traffic of over 250,000 customers.

Exercise 9

1 You want to get a conversation started. You could say:
Where exactly are you from, if I may ask? 2 You want to

avoid a misunderstanding and elicit further information. You could say: *So we're talking about half past five. Could you give me more details about the restaurant?* 3 You want to elicit information about the visitor's special needs. You could say: *I see you've been looking at … And so you have an interest in…?*
4 You want to avoid a misunderstanding. You could say: *Sorry, I didn't quite get that. I'm not very familiar with China. Would you mind repeating the names of the towns?*

Exercise 10

1 f 2 f 3 f 4 f 5 t

Evasive Talk

I was just trying to get a general impression of what's new on the market. | Well, you might say that we're into environmental technology, too. | I'm afraid that I can't give you an answer off the top of my head. | I'll have to check my diary and get back to you. | Well, if you don't mind, I'll just take one of these catalogues with me and get back to you later.

Exercise 12

Possible answers:

1 I'm just trying to get an idea of what's out there, at this stage. 2 I'm in the … industry. 3 I'm afraid I'm not very well informed about that. 4 Why don't you leave your card and I'll get back to you when things have quieted down.

Exercise 13

Intercultural obstacles in order of appearance

1 dietary restrictions due to religious beliefs 2 position/role of women 3 significance of family ties 4 marriage customs

Exercise 2

1 issues 2 unpredictable 3 favor 4 agent on site
5 red tape 6 mirror 7 get in touch with

Exercise 3

The speakers mention

local companies being preferred to foreign ones | trouble with paperwork | authorities and legal issues | adhering to deadlines | quality management

Exercise 5

Dear Thomas,

Thanks for the sales report for Q1. Great job. Although the figures don't look that bad, I think we have to **reduce** labor costs and **gain** new market segments. My feeling is that we should **accelerate** things with China Ware. They're also **participating** in the Home Living Trade Fair in April.

Please **contact** Luan Zhang to make an appointment. The agenda should include the following:

· Exploration of market opportunities: What chances does the market offer? Should we mainly **focus on** the Zhejiang area?
· Quality Management system – how can we make sure European/German quality and safety standards are **maintained**?
· Sales team: Is there are trained sales team, sales support?
· Can we **cooperate** with regional distributors?
· What are the territorial restrictions?
· Would China Ware be interested in **forming** a strategic partnership?

You may want to ask Rita Gao to join you for the talk.

Please keep me **informed**.

Thanks,
Oliver Lücke

Exercise 6

explore market opportunities | maintain quality standards | work together with regional distributors | check out a manufacturing site | form a strategic partnership | contact the sales team | set up a quality management system

Exercise 8

Welcoming and exchanging pleasantries

Good morning, my name is Thomas Baker from Gärtner Life. | We have an appointment with Luan Zhang. | Certainly, sir. | Luan Zhang is expecting you. | Let me show you to our meeting area. | Welcome to China Ware. | My name is Luan Zhang. | It's a pleasure to finally meet you in person. | Let me introduce you to my colleague Rita Gao. | Nice to meet you, here is my card. | It's a pleasure to meet you, too. | Ms Gao, if I may ask, are you from China?

Exercise 10

S   We would be particularly interested in …
P   I'm convinced that …
S   As you probably know …
S   Could you imagine …
S   What I actually had in mind …
S   May I propose that …
S   We would be more than delighted …
P   May I present you with …
P   It has been a real pleasure …

Exercise 12

Issues in the conversation

Sales figures look quite good for the 3rd quarter. However, sales in small shops have decreased. A solution in proposed.

1 Shall we move on to business? 2 How's business at …?
3 Why do you think that is? 4 Right. I can see your point.
5 What do you suggest we should do? 6. Sounds like a good idea.

Exercise 13

Issues mentioned:

Problems with the last advertising campaign. | Promotional material didn't arrive on time. | It arrived way after the Christmas sales had begun. It was supposed to arrive before. | There were mistakes in the technical data sheets. | The Polish translation was inadequate. | Too many people are involved.

1 c 2 e 3 f 4 a 5 d 6 b

Exercise 14

More appropriate answers

1 There are some issues with the campaign. 2 I have another commitment. 3 I'm not happy with the way this has been handled. 4 What exactly seems to be the problem? 5 Why don't we arrange another meeting? 6 I will sort this out and get back to you as soon as I have found out what happened.

Exercise 17

Ms Bertani's preconceptions regarding German producers of coffee makers are that their products are less suited for baristas and gourmet coffee shops.

1 admit 2 target groups 3 compete 4 expire 5 As to the quantities 6 flexible 7 sketch out conditions | a first draft before we get down to the nitty-gritty

Exercise 18

1 c 2 e 3 d 4 b 5 a

Unit 6

Warm-Up

1 k 2 d 3 j 4 g 5 a 6 h 7 e 8 c 9 b 10 f 11 i

Exercise 1

1 B, C 2 B, A 3 A 4 B 5 A, B 6 The writer of mentions meeting the recipient at the trade fair and what they talked about.

Exercise 2

More formal follow-up phrases

Say hello to: my best regards to … | Please let me know what you think: I look forward to hearing from you | I could arrange another appointment: I could easily reschedule | … as soon as possible: at your earliest convenience | We still have to talk about the terms …: conditions would still have to be negotiated | It was nice to …: it was a pleasure | I went ahead and wrote up: I have taken the liberty of drafting | They thought your suggestions were good: your proposal has been met with enthusiasm

Exercise 3

Expressions of reference

As mentioned in …, | As I mentioned | As promised | As to the proposed cooperation | Further to our conversation on … | As we were saying, | As far as … is concerned, | With respect to | Concerning

Exercise 4

1 As I was saying 2 Further to 3 As far as … is concerned
4 As to 5 Concerning / with respect to 6 as promised

Exercise 5

1 As I was saying, this is only one model in a very wide range.
2 Just in case you would like to arrange an appointment with one of our representatives, please call Samantha Evans at the number below. 3 I am taking the liberty of attaching our latest price list and catalogue. 4 Thanks very much for visiting our exhibit at the recent show in Frankfurt. 5 I am confident that you will be able to find one that meets your needs. 6 It was a pleasure to be able to demonstrate our state-of-the-art food processor of which we are especially proud.

Exercise 6

How much I appreciated | I especially enjoyed | lovely | talented | the chance | fitting conclusion | mutually satisfying agreement | looking forward to | how much I enjoyed

Exercise 7

1 This is just a note to say how much I enjoyed the sightseeing tour of your city. 2 I especially / really / certainly hope that you had a pleasant return journey. 3 It was a great pleasure to be able to talk to you again last week. 4 I sincerely hope that you had a pleasant return journey. 5 We would be honored to have the opportunity to entertain you again.

Exercise 10

1 To check if he has received the catalogue and would be interested in a visit. 2 He hasn't had time. There was a backlog of work. 3 If Gärtner has a showroom nearby.

Exercise 11

1 I just wanted to check that you received our catalogue.
2 You expressed a special interest in … 3 I hope you've had time to consider our offer. 4 It would be no trouble to bring the machines to your office. 5 When would it be a convenient time for you?

Exercise 13

Organization | Technical support | International customers | Visitor traffic | Booth maintenance | Catering facilities | Security

Useful Phrases

The phrases below are useful tools in and around the show. Highlight phrases which are particulary relevant to you and add phrases that you've experienced as helpful.

Getting in touch

Inviting customers

We would be delighted if you joined us …
We look forward to seeing you at …
You can sign up for …
We are particularly excited about our latest …
Our products will be on display.
Please do arrange a personal meeting …
The fair will bring together …

Greeting and welcoming

Please, come in.
How are you today?
What can I do for you?
Let me know if you need any help.
I'd be happy tp demonstrate / to show you …
Feel free to look around.

Making arrangements

When would be a good time for …
Would this afternoon/this Monday … be convenient?
Are you available this …
How about later/earlier …

Striking up a conversation

I see you're from …
I'd like to introduce you to …/myself …
Is anyone sitting here?
I couldn't help noticing …
Can I get you …

Asking for and giving directions

I'm sorry, I seem to be lost…
I've lost my bearings …
Could you give me a landmark of some kind?
You nearly there.
Take the left into the aisle…
Take the escalator …
We're in the corner booth …

Responses

That's very impressive.
Pleased to meet you.
That's a coincidence.
Do you happen to have a card?
How about getting together …
I'd love to!

Promoting and presenting

Promoting products

We actually specialize in …
The … was a revolution …
We are particularly excited about …
It will make a great addition to your …
This is our latest range of …
It will provide you with …

Describing trends

Our expectations were exceeded.
Rocketing stand costs trouble exhibitors.
In May share prices have reached a peak.
Prices are levelling out.
Trade Fair Services have reached a new low.
There was a sharp slump in prices.

Highlighting information

I'd like to point out that …
You might be interested in …
Maybe you'd like to have a look at …

Giving new information

Let me give you an idea of what …
I'd now like to draw your attention to …
Let me talk you through …

Opening

First of all, let me thank you all for coming
here today.
It's a pleasure to welcome you today.
It's good to see you all here.
Let me introduce myself. I'm …
I feel ashamed for having to do this in English.

Clarifying a point

To continue with what I was saying …
What I meant was …
What I was saying was …

Introducing your topic

What I'd like to talk about is …
I'm here to present …
Today I'm going to talk about …
By the end of the talk you will be familiar with …

Summarizing

To put it all in a nutshell …
What this all boild down to…
To sum things up …
In conclusion …

Conflicts and solutions

Making complaints

I'm very concerned about …
We were assured that the …
I'm sorry to bother you, but …
We're having trouble …
Something went wrong with …
There seems to be a problem with …

Offering solutions to problems

You mentioned certain issues that …
I fully understand …
Is there anything (else) I could do …
I suggest that you …
Just a sec. I'll have a look (at the computer).
I will certainly sort this out.
That should do the job.

Clarifying things

I have to admit…
I was under the impression that …
I'm well aware of …
As you probably know …
As I have already explained …
We were thinking of …
I'd prefer to reconsider …

Evasive talk

I'm just trying to get a feel for what's out there before I make any decisions.
Let me get back to you later on that.
Unfortunately, I'm tied up for the rest of the …
May I take a brochure instead?
I'd like to get an overview first …
It's still up in the air/undecided.
Sorry, it looks like I've got an urgent call.

Calming people

I can sympathize completely.
I'd like to apologize for the inconvenience.
I'm (terribly) sorry to hear that …
I'm confident he/she wants to …

Insisting

We were assured that …
Would you mind doing that immediately?
We must insist that …
We'd appreciate it if you could …

Business dealings

Expressing an interest

How's business at ...?
We would be particularly interested in ...
When would be a good time for an appointment so you could tell me a little bit more?
We would appreciate it if you ...

Making an offer

Could you imagine...
May I propose that ...
We would be more than delighted if you ...
We would be particulary interested in ...

Offering hospitality / Presenting a gift

Would you care to join us for some tea?
Lunch is on us.
May we present you with ...?
May I present you with ...

Expressing thanks

It's been a real pleasure...
This is very generous of you.

Following up on the show

Thank you again for the pleasant ...
I was especially honored to ...
At the show you expressed a special interest in ...
Further to our conversation on ...
I just wanted to check that you received (our catalogue).
I have taken the liberty of drafting ...
Your proposal has been met with enthusiasm.
It would be no trouble to ...
I'm confident that we will ...

A–Z Wordlist

A

above   oben genannt
to accelerate   beschleunigen
to access sth   auf etw zugreifen
access   Zugang, Zugriff, Zufahrt
access, vehicle ~   Zufahrt
accessible   erreichbar, zugänglich
according to   nach, zufolge
account   Konto
account, to take sth into ~   etw berücksichtigen
to accumulate   sich ansammeln, sich anhäufen
accurate   genau
to achieve   erreichen
to acquire   erwerben
to act   fungieren
to adapt   (sich) anpassen
adaptor   Adapter
addition   Ergänzung
addition, in ~   außerdem
adequate   angemessen
to adhere to sth   sich an etw halten, etw einhalten
adherence   Einhaltung
to adjust   einstellen
to admit   zugeben, eingestehen
to advance sth   etw voranbringen
advance, in ~   im Voraus
advance payment   Vorauszahlung, Anzahlung
advertising   Werbung, Werbe-
to advise   raten, beraten
to affect sth   sich auf etw auswirken
affordable   erschwinglich
after-sales service   Kundendienst, Kundenservice
agent   Händler/in, Repräsentant/in, Vertreter/in
agile   beweglich, flexibel
agreement   Vereinbarung, Vertrag, Übereinkunft
to aim at sth   auf etw abzielen, etw bezwecken
air, up in the ~   in der Schwebe, ungewiss
aisle   Gang
all-time high   historischer Höchststand
alongside   neben
amazing   erstaunlich
amplifier   Verstärker
annex   Nebengebäude
annoying   nervig, nervend, ärgerlich
to anticipate   vorhersehen
anticipation   Erwartung
apart from   abgesehen von, außer
to apologize   sich entschuldigen
apparently   anscheinend
appealing   ansprechend, attraktiv

to appear   auftreten, vorkommen, erscheinen, scheinen
appliance, electrical ~   Elektrogerät
appliances, household ~   Haushaltsgeräte
to appoint   ernennen, bestimmen
appointment   Termin
appointment book *(AE)*   Terminkalender
to appreciate   zu schätzen wissen, verstehen, sich (einer Sache) bewusst sein, anerkennen
appreciation   Wertschätzung, Anerkennung
approach   Herangehensweise
to approach sb   an jdn herantreten, auf jdn zugehen
appropriate   passend
approval   Genehmigung, Zustimmung
to approve   genehmigen
approximately   ungefähr, zirka
to arrange   *(Termin)* ausmachen, vereinbaren
to arrange for sth   etw veranlassen, für etw sorgen
ashamed, to feel ~   sich schämen
assignment   Arbeitsauftrag
assistance   Hilfe, Unterstützung
to associate sth with sth   etw mit etw in Verbindung bringen
to assume   annehmen, vermuten, unterstellen
to assume a position   eine Stellung einnehmen, eine Postition bekleiden
assumption   Unterstellung
to assure sb sth   jdm etw zusichern
astounding   erstaunlich
to attach   beilegen
to attend sth   an etw teilnehmen, etw besuchen
attendance   Teilnahme, Anwesenheit
attendee   Teilnehmer/in, Besucher/in
attention span   Aufmerksamkeitsspanne
attitude   Einstellung, Haltung
to attract sb   jdn anlocken
audience   Publikum
audience, target ~   Zielgruppe
audio equipment   Tonanlage, Audiogeräte
authorities   Behörden
authority   Kapazität, Experte/-in
availability   Verfügbarkeit
to avoid   vermeiden
awake   wach
awaited, eagerly ~   mit Spannung erwartet

award   Preis, Auszeichnung
aware, to be ~ of sth   sich einer Sache bewusst sein

B

background noise   Hintergrundgeräusche
backlog   Arbeitsrückstand
battery   Akku, Batterie
battle   Schlacht
bay   Bucht
beam, cross ~   Traverse
to bear sth in mind   an etw denken
bearings, to get one's ~   sich orientieren
bearings, to lose one's ~   die Orientierung verlieren
beforehand   vorher, im Voraus
behalf, on ~ of sb   in jds Auftrag, in jds Namen
behind the scenes   hinter den Kulissen
Belarus   Weißrussland
belt, conveyor ~   Förderband
benefit   Vorteil, Nutzen, Pluspunkt
to benefit from sth   von etw profitieren
best practice   beispielhafte Verfahren
beyond   jenseits, außerhalb
bilingual   zweisprachig
blender   Mixer
to blow sth   etw platzen lassen
to board   an Bord gehen
to boil down to sth   auf etw hinauslaufen
to boost   ankurbeln
booth   Stand
booth staffer   Standmitarbeiter/in
to bother sb   jdn stören, jdn belästigen
brain, to pick sb's ~s   jdn ausfragen, jdn ausquetschen
branch   Niederlassung; Sparte
brand new   brandneu
branding   Markenentwicklung, Markenaufbau
to break down   kaputtgehen, zusammenbrechen
to break new ground   Neuland betreten
breakaway compactor   stationäre Verdichtungsanlage
to bring sth along   etw mitbringen
to broaden   erweitern
brochure   Prospekt
to browse   stöbern
buddy   Kumpel
bulk order   Großbestellung
bulky   klobig

to **bump into sb**   jdn zufällig
   treffen
bureaucracy   Bürokratie
business card   Visitenkarte
business dealings
   Geschäftsbeziehungen, Geschäfte
business veteran   altgediente/r,
   erfahrene/r Geschäftsmann/-frau
buying power   Kaufkraft

C

cable car   Seilbahn
cable   Kabel
to **calculate**   kalkulieren, rechnen
calculation, mixed ~
   Mischkalkulation
call retrieval   Gesprächsannahme,
   Gesprächsabruf
to **calm**   beruhigen
campaign   (Werbe-)Kampagne
capabilty   Möglichkeit, Fähigkeit,
   Funktion
capacity   Kapazität
carpet   Teppich
carpeting   Teppichboden
to **cart**   karren
case   Kasten; Fall
case, just in ~   für alle Fälle
casual   locker, ungezwungen,
   beiläufig
catalogue   Katalog
to **catch up on sth**   etw nachholen
to **catch up with sb**   jdn erwischen
to **cater for sth**   auf etw eingehen,
   einer Sache gerecht werden
catering personnel   Servierkräfte
catering supplies
   Gastronomiebedarf
to **cause**   verursachen
chain   Kette
to **challenge**   herausfordern
channel   Kanal, Weg
charge, in ~ of sth   zuständig für
   etw
to **check sth out**   sich etw ansehen
to **clarify**   klären
clarity   Deutlichkeit, Klarheit,
   Verständlichkeit
clay pot   Tontopf
cleaning staff   Reinigungskräfte
clearance height   lichte Höhe
clipboard   Klemmbrett
clockwork, to run like ~   wie am
   Schnürchen laufen
clogged   verstopft
to **coax sth out of sb**   jdm etw
   abschwatzen
coffee maker   Kaffeemaschine
coincidence   Zufall
to **come apart**   auseinanderfallen
to **come up with sth**   sich etw
   ausdenken, sich etw einfallen
   lassen
come rain or shine   in guten wie
   in schlechten Zeiten
commencement   Beginn der
   Vertragsverhandlungen
commercial   gewerblich

to **commit sth to memory**
   etw auswendig lernen
commitment   Verpflichtung
common ground, to find ~
   eine gemeinsame Basis finden
community   Gemeinschaft,
   Gemeinde
compaction system
   Verdichtungssystem
compactor   Verdichter
compactor, breakaway ~
   stationäre Verdichtungsanlage
competitive prices   günstige
   Preise
competitor   Konkurrent/in,
   Wettbewerber, Konkurrenz
complaint   Beschwerde
complement   Ergänzung
completion of a contract
   Vertragsabschluss
complimentary ticket   Freikarte
comprehensive   umfassend
compressed-air   Druckluft
to **compromise**   Kompromisse
   eingehen
concern, no need for ~
   kein Grund zur Sorge
to **concern**   betreffen
concierge services   Portierdienst,
   Hausmeisterservice
conclusion   Abschluss
condition   Bedingung,
   Voraussetzung
conditions   Konditionen
conferencing   Konferenztechnik
confident   überzeugt,
   zuversichtlich
configuration   Ausstattung,
   Gestaltung
to **confirm**   bestätigen
to **confuse**   verwechseln
conjunction, in ~ with   in
   Verbindung mit, in Zusamenarbeit
   mit
connection   Verbindung, Leitung
consecutive   aufeinanderfolgend
to **consider**   berücksichtigen, in
   Betracht ziehen, in Erwägung
   ziehen
to **consider sth sth**   etw für etw
   halten
to **consolidate**   zusammenführen
consultant   Berater/in
contingency plan   Plan B
contract   Vertrag
convenience, at your earliest ~
   sobald es Ihnen möglich ist
convenient   passend, günstig
conveniently   günstig
convention   Tagung, Konferenz,
   Zusammenkunft
conveyor belt   Förderband
conveyor technology
   Fördertechnik
to **convince**   überzeugen
cookware   Kochgeschirr
coolant   Kühlmittel
corner stand   Eckstand

costly   kostspielig
counter   Theke, Tresen
course of action   Vorgehensweise
cover   Hülle
to **cover**   abdecken; (Thema etc.)
   behandeln
cross beam   Traverse
cross-cultural   interkulturell,
   kulturübergreifend
cross-industry
   branchenübergreifend
crowd gatherer   Promoter;
   Publikumsmagnet
crystal ball   Kristallkugel
C-suite   Vorstandsetage, Chefetage
to **cultivate**   pflegen, kultivieren
custom   Sitte, Brauch
customer relations
   Kundenbeziehungen
customer service   Kundendienst
to **customize**   individuell anpassen
to **cut**   kürzen, reduzieren
to **cut costs**   Kosten senken
to **cut down on sth**   etw senken,
   etw reduzieren
cutlery   Besteck
cutlery, disposable ~
   Einwegbesteck

D

dairy products   Milchprodukte
to **dare**   (es) wagen
data projector   Beamer
deadline   Frist
dealings, business ~
   Geschäftsbeziehungen, Geschäfte
dear, to be ~ to sb   jdm am Herzen
   liegen
to **debrief sb**   mit jdm etw
   nachbesprechen
decision maker
   Entscheidungsträger
to **decline**   zurückgehen,
   abnehmen
decrease   Rückgang
to **decrease**   sinken, zurückgehen,
   abnehmen
dedicated   engagiert
to **deem sth sth**   etw für etw
   halten/erachten
default   Standard
to **delay**   verzögern
delayed, to be ~   sich verspäten
delighted   erfreut
delighted, to be ~   sich freuen
delivery period   Lieferfrist
demand, to place ~s on sb
   Anforderungen an jdn stellen
to **demonstrate**   vorführen
demonstration   Vorführung
to **depart**   abfahren, ablegen
to **depend on sth**   von etw
   abhängen
deprived of   ohne
designated   ausgewiesen
desired, to leave sth to be ~
   etw zu wünschen übrig lassen
despite   trotz

to **destroy**   zerstören
to **detect sth**   erkennen, entdecken
to **determine**   bestimmen
to **develop**   entwickeln
development   Entwicklung
device   Gerät
to **devote**   widmen
diary *(BE)*   Terminkalender
dietary restrictions
   Ernährungsvorschriften,
   -einschränkungen
diligent   gewissenhaft, fleißig
dim   schwach, düster
disappointment   Enttäuschung
disaster   Katastrophe
to **discharge**   ableiten, abladen
to **disclose**   preisgeben
discount   Rabatt
to **discover**   entdecken
to **dismantle**   abbauen,
   abmontieren
to **display**   zeigen, ausstellen
display, on ~   ausgestellt
display case   Display, Aufsteller
disposable cutlery   Einwegbesteck
disposable income   verfügbares
   Einkommen
distinctive features
   besondere Kennzeichen,
   Unterscheidungsmerkmale
to **distribute**   vertreiben, liefern,
   verteilen
distribution   Vertrieb, Verteilung
distribution channel
   Vertriebskanal
distributor   Zwischenhändler
diversity   Vielfalt
division   Abteilung, Sparte
double-digit   zweistellig
doubt   Zweifel
doubt, no ~   zweifellos
downturn, economic ~
   Konjunkturabschwung,
   Wirtschaftsflaute, Abschwung
draft   Entwurf
to **draft**   *(Text)* entwerfen,
   formulieren, aufsetzen
drain   Abfluss, Ablauf, Belastung,
   Aufwand
drainable   entwässerbar
draped stand-up table   Stehtisch
   mit Husse
to **draw**   ziehen, zeichnen
due, to be ~ to sth   an etw liegen
due, to be ~ to do sth   etw
   demnächst tun sollen
due to   aufgrund von
durable   strapazierfähig
duty roster   Dienstplan

E

eager, to be ~ to do sth   etw
   unbedingt tun wollen
eagerly awaited   mit Spannung
   erwartet
easel   Staffelei
easy maintenance
   Wartungsfreundlichkeit

easy-to-handle   einfach im
   Gebrauch, einfach zu bedienen
economic downturn
   Konjunkturabschwung,
   Wirtschaftsflaute, Abschwung
efficient   effizient
efforts   Bemühungen,
   Anstrengungen
electrical appliance   Elektrogerät
electricity   Strom
element, out of your ~   fehl am
   Platz
to **elicit information**
   Informationen entlocken/erlangen
embarrassing   peinlich
to **embrace sth**   etw annehmen
to **emphasize**   betonen
to **employ sth**   etw anwenden, etw
   einsetzen
empowered   befugt, berechtigt
to **enable sb to do sth**   es jdm
   ermöglichen, etw zu tun
to **encounter**   begegnen
end stand   Kopfstand
endurance   Ausdauer
to **engage sb in a conversation**
   jdn in ein Gespräch verwickeln
to **engrave**   gravieren, eingravieren
to **enhance**   verbessern
to **enquire about sth**   sich nach
   etw erkundigen, sich über etw
   informieren
enquiry   Anfrage
to **ensure**   gewährleisten
to **enter**   betreten, eintreten
entertaining   *hier:* Bewirtung *(von
   Geschäftspartnern)*
to **entitle**   berechtigen
entrance strategy
   Eintrittsstrategie, Zugangsstrategie
entrance   Eingang
entrepreneur   Unternehmer/in
environment   Umfeld, Umgebung
environmental technology
   Umwelttechnik
to **equip**   ausstatten, ausrüsten
equipment   Ausrüstung, Geräte
equipped   ausgestattet
escalator   Rolltreppe
essential   wichtig, unerlässlich
to **establish contact**   Kontakt
   aufnehmen
to **estimate**   schätzen
ethnic group   Volksgruppe
etiquette   Etikette,
   Verhaltensregel(n)
evaluation   Auswertung
evasive   ausweichend
event   Veranstaltung
to **exceed**   übertreffen, übersteigen
excited   begeistert
exciting   spannend, aufregend
exclamation mark   Ausrufezeichen
exclusive right   Exklusivrecht
exclusive right of sale
   Alleinverkaufsrecht
exercise bike   Trainingsfahrrad
to **exhibit**   ausstellen

exhibit   Ausstellungsstück
exhibition   Ausstellung, Messe
exhibition grounds
   Ausstellungsgelände,
   Messegelände
exhibition site
   Ausstellungsgelände,
   Messegelände
exhibitor   Aussteller/in
exit strategy   Rückzugsstrategie
to **expand on sth**   auf etw näher/
   im Detail eingehen
expenses   Kosten, Spesen,
   Aufwendungen
to **experience**   erleben
expertise   Fachwissen, Kompetenz
to **expire**   *(Vertrag etc.:)* auslaufen,
   ablaufen
to **explore**   sondieren, prüfen
exploration   Sondierung
to **express**   ausdrücken
extension cable/cord
   Verlängerungskabel/-schnur
extinguisher   Feuerlöscher
eye contact   Blickkontakt

F

fabric   Stoff
to **facilitate**   erleichtern,
   begünstigen
facilitator   Moderator/in,
   Seminarleiter/in
facilities   Einrichtungen
facilities, production ~
   Produktionsanlagen
to **fail**   ein Misserfolg sein
failure   Fehlschlag, Schwachpunkt
fair grounds   Messegelände
familiar   vertraut
to **fancy, Can you ~ that?**
   Kaum zu glauben, oder?
faraway   weit entfernt, entlegen
to **favor**   bevorzugen, favorisieren
feature   (Produkt-)Merkmal,
   (Produkt-)Eigenschaft
figures   Zahlen
to **fill sb in**   jdn über etw ins Bild
   setzen
filthy   schmutzig
to **finalize sth**   etw endgültig
   festlegen
to **fire away**   losschießen
fire extinguisher   Feuerlöscher
first-hand   persönlich, hautnah,
   aus erster Hand
fit   Passform
fitter   Monteur/in
fitting   passend, angemessen
to **fix**   reparieren, regeln
fixed   fest
flash flooding   plötzliche
   Überschwemmung, Sturzflut
flask   Trinkflasche
floor load   Bodentragfähigkeit
floor plan   Grundriss
flooring   Fußboden
fluent, to be ~ (in a language)
   (eine Sprache) fließend sprechen

folder   Ordner
folding chair   Klappstuhl
to **follow up on sth**   etw weiterverfolgen
follow-up   Nachfassen, Nachfassaktion
food processor   Küchenmaschine
footprint   Fußabdruck
forklift   Gabelstapler
form   Formular
formalized   formalisiert
former   ehemalig
to **forward**   weiterleiten
to **foster**   fördern, pflegen
foundation   Basis, Fundament
fountain   Brunnen
frankly speaking   offen gesagt
freebie   Werbegeschenk
fridge   Kühlschrank
functionality   Funktionstüchtigkeit, Funktionsvielfalt
furnishings   Ausstattung, Einrichtung
further, to take it (even) ~   noch weitergehen (als)
further to …   was … betrifft
furthermore   darüber hinaus, außerdem
fuss   Aufregung, Brimborium, Aufheben

G

gadget   Gerät
gaffer tape   Gewebeband
to **gain**   gewinnen, erwerben
garbage (AE)   Müll, Abfall
gate   Tor, Einfahrt
to **gather sth from sth**   etw aus etw ersehen
gathering   Zusammenkunft, Treffen
gear   Kleidung
gender   Geschlecht
generosity   Großzügigkeit
generous   großzügig
to **get back to sb**   sich bei jdm (zurück)melden
get-together   Treffen
giveaway   Werbegeschenk
glitch   Panne
glue   *hier:* Kitt
to **go out of one's way**   sich besondere Mühe geben, etw zu tun
go-ahead, to give the ~   grünes Licht geben
good/great value (for money)   (sehr) preisgünstig, (sehr) preiswert
grain-fed beef   Rindfleisch aus Getreideaufzucht
to **grant**   einräumen, gewähren
gravel   Kies
ground, to break new ~   Neuland betreten
ground, to find common ~   eine gemeinsame Basis finden
ground plan   Grundriss

grounds, exhibition ~   Ausstellungsgelände, Messegelände
grounds, fair ~   Messegelände
growth   Wachstum
growth rate   Zuwachsrate, Wachstumsrate
to **guarantee**   garantieren
to **guard**   bewachen
gym   Fitnessstudio

H

hall   Halle, Saal
to **handle**   umgehen, erledigen, behandeln, handhaben
handling   Bedienung
handshake   Handschlag, Händeschütteln
harbor   Hafen
hard-wearing   robust
hasty   eilig, hastig, übereilt
head, off the top of my ~   spontan
head, to make ~ or tail of sth   aus etw schlau werden
headed, to be ~ for   unterwegs sein nach
headquarters   Zentrale
healthy   gesund
heckler   Zwischenrufer
heel lock   fester Fersensitz
high street (BE)   Hauptgeschäftsstraße
high table   Stehtisch
high   Höchststand
high, all-time ~   historischer Höchststand
to **highlight**   hervorheben, betonen
high-pressure cooker   Schnellkochtopf
hiking boots   Wanderstiefel
to **hire**   engagieren, anstellen
honest, to be ~   ehrlich gesagt
honorable   ehrenwert
honored   geehrt
hook   Haken
to **hook up**   anschließen
hospitality   Bewirtung von Gästen
host   Gastgeber
to **host**   (Veranstaltung) ausrichten
household appliances   Haushaltsgeräte

I

ignorance   Unkenntnis, Unwissen
immediate   unmittelbar; nächste/r/s
immediately   unverzüglich, sofort
impact   Auswirkungen
importance, of utmost ~   von allergrößter Bedeutung
impression, to be under the ~ that   den Eindruck haben, dass
impressive   beeindruckend
to **improve**   verbessern, sich bessern
improvised   improvisiert

inadequate   unzulänglich, unzureichend
to **include**   einschließen
income   Einkommen, Einkünfte
inconvenience   Unannehmlichkeiten
incredible   unglaublich, sagenhaft
to **incur**   (Kosten:) anfallen
to **indicate**   andeuten
to **indulge in sth**   sich in etw ergehen
industry   Branche, Industrie
industry knowledge   Branchenwissen
influence   Einfluss
ingenuity   Einfallsreichtum
inhabitant   Einwohner
to **initiate**   einleiten, anstoßen, initiieren
insight   Erkenntnis
to **insist**   darauf bestehen, beteuern
instant   sofortig
insurance   Versicherung
intangible   nicht greifbar
interaction   Zusammenspiel, Wechselwirkung
interlinking   miteinander verbunden
intriguing   faszinierend, hochinteressant
to **introduce sb**   jdn vorstellen
introvert   introvertierter Mensch
intrusive   aufdringlich, penetrant
to **invest**   investieren
invitation   Einladung
to **invite**   einladen, auffordern, erbitten
invite   Einladung
invitee   eingeladene/r Teilnehmer/in
involved   beteiligt, (Kosten, Aufwand:) anfallend
to **iron sth out**   etw ausbügeln
island stand   Inselstand
issue   Thema, Frage, Problem
issue, open ~   ungelöstes Problem
item   Artikel, Gegenstand

J

jammed   blockiert
jobless   arbeitslos
to **join sb**   jdn besuchen, zu jdm kommen
to **jot sth down**   etw aufschreiben, etw notieren
just in case   für alle Fälle

K

key   Haupt-, wichtigste/r/s
keynote speaker   Hauptredner/in
to **kid, You must be kidding.**   Nicht im Ernst!
kit   Set

L

to label   etikettieren, beschriften
labor costs   Lohnkosten, Arbeitskosten
lack   Mangel, Fehlen
landline   Festnetzanschluss
landmark   Orientierungspunkt
largely   größtenteils, hauptsächlich
lasting   dauerhaft
late, to run ~   spät dran sein
launch   Start, Produkteinführung
to launch   starten, *(Produkt:)* einführen
lead   Geschäftskontakt, Lead
lead form   Lead-Formular
lead management   Lead-Management *(Verwaltung von Geschäftskontakten)*
leading figures   führende Persönlichkeiten
to leaf trough sth   etw durchblättern
to learn the ropes   sich einarbeiten, etw in den Griff bekommen
least, not ~   nicht zuletzt
leather   Leder
leather upper   Oberleder
to leave sth to be desired   etw zu wünschen übrig lassen
legal jungle   Gesetzesdickicht, Paragraphendschungel
legal   gesetzlich, rechtlich
level   Ebene, Niveau
liberty, to take the ~ of doing sth   sich erlauben, etw zu tun
license agreement   Lizenzvereinbarung, Lizenzvertrag
license partner   Lizenzpartner
licensee   Lizenznehmer
light bulb   Glühbirne
light fixtures   Belechtungselemente, Leuchten
lighting   Beleuchtung
limited   begrenzt, beschränkt
line (of business)   Branche
liner   Futter
the lion's den   die Höhle des Löwen
literature stand   Prospektständer
load   Last
to load   laden, verladen
location   Standort
lock   Schloss
locker   Schließfach
logistics   Logistik
long-term   langfristig
loop, to keep sb in the ~   jdn auf dem Laufenden halten
lost, to get ~   verloren gehen
loudspeaker   Lautsprecher
lounge   Salon
low   Tiefststand
low-key   unauffällig
lubricant   Schmiermittel
to lure   locken
luxury   Luxus(-)

M

mad house   Irrenhaus
to maintain   einhalten, aufrecht erhalten
maintenance   Wartung
maintenance, easy ~   Wartungsfreundlichkeit
major   groß, wichtig, bedeutend, Haupt-
make   Marke, Fabrikat
to make sure   dafür sorgen, gewährleisten, sicherstellen
to make the most of sth   etw optimal ausnutzen, das Beste aus etw machen
to man   *(Posten, etc.:)* besetzen
to manage sth   etw regeln
manufacturer   Hersteller
manufacturing   Fertigung, Herstellung, Fabrikation
manufacturing site   Produktionsstätte
market research   Marktforschung
market segment   Marktsegment
mark-up   Aufschlag, Preiserhöhung
matinee   Nachmittagsveranstaltung
matter   Angelegenheit, Frage
matter, no ~   ganz egal, ganz gleich
to maximize   maximieren
means   Mittel, Möglichkeit
meantime, in the ~   in der Zwischenzeit
measures   Maßnahmen
to meet sb's needs   jds Bedürfnissen entsprechen
to meet standards   Ansprüche/Maßstäbe erfüllen
to mention, not to ~   ganz zu schweigen von
merely   lediglich, nur
mess, to make a complete ~ out of sth   etw völlig gegen die Wand fahren
microphone; mike   Mikrofon; Mikro
microphone, noise-cancelling ~   Mikrofon mit Störschallunterdrückung
to mind doing sth   etw dagegen haben, etw zu tun
mind you   allerdings
to mirror   widerspiegeln
mistaken, to be ~   sich irren
misunderstanding   Missverständnis
mixed calculation   Mischkalkulation
mixed-up   durcheinander
mixer   Rührgerät
momentum   Dynamik, Entwicklung
to monitor   überwachen
mourning   Trauer
municipal   kommunal

municipality   Kommune, Gemeinde
muscle   Muskel
mutually   gegenseitig, für beide Seiten

N

napkin   Serviette
to negotiate   verhandeln
niceties   Nettigkeiten
niche market   Nischenmarkt
nitty-gritty, to get down to the ~   ans Eingemachte gehen, ins Detail gehen
no doubt   zweifellos
no matter   ganz egal, ganz gleich
noise   Geräusch, Lärm
noise-cancelling microphone   Mikrofon mit Störschallunterdrückung
noisy   laut
non-committal   unverbindlich
non-stick pan   antihaftbeschichtete Pfanne
not least   nicht zuletzt
not to mention ...   ganz zu schweigen von …
notion   Vorstellung, Konzept, Begriff
nutshell, to put it in a ~   kurz gesagt

O

observer   Beobachter/in
obstacle   Hürde, Hindernis
to obtain   erhalten, bekommen
to offend sb   jdn brüskieren, jdn beleidigen
on site   vor Ort
open issue   ungelöstes Problem
to operate   geschäftlich tätig sein
operation   Betrieb, Geschäft, Unternehmen
operational procedures   Betriebsablauf, Betriebsverfahren
opportunity   Chance, Gelegenheit, Möglichkeit
to optimize   optimieren
order form   Auftragsformular
order   Auftrag, Bestellung
order, bulk ~   Großbestellung
order, to place an ~   einen Auftrag erteilen, eine Bestellung aufgeben
organizer   Veranstalter/in, Organisator/in
otherwise   sonst
ought to   sollen
outcome   Ergebnis
outlet *(AE)*   Steckdose
outlet, power ~   Stromanschluss, Steckdose
to outnumber   übersteigen, übertreffen
to outsource   auslagern
outstanding   hervorragend, überragend
over the top   übertrieben

overall impression Gesamteindruck
to **overhear** zufällig mithören
overpriced zu teuer
overtime Überstunden
overview Überblick, Übersicht

P

pack load Belastung
package Angebotspaket, Pauschalangebot
paint residue Farbreste
to **pair** paaren, verbinden
pan, non-stick ~ antihaftbeschichtete Pfanne
pan, steel ~ Stahlpfanne
paramount von größter Wichtigkeit
parity Gleichheit
participant Teilnehmer/in
participation Teilnahme
particular speziell
particularly besonders
partly teilweise
patented design patentierte Konstruktion
patience Geduld
pattern Muster
to **pay off** sich auszahlen
peak Höchststand
peer learning kollegiales Lernen, Wissensaustausch unter Kollegen
to **perceive** wahrnehmen
permanently dauerhaft, endgültig
permit Genehmigung, Erlaubnis
to **permit** erlauben, gestatten
personal space persönliche Distanzzone
personnel Personal
to **pick sb's brains** jdn ausfragen, jdn ausquetschen
pickpocket Taschendieb
picture rail Bilderschiene
pinch, in a ~ im Notfall
pitch Angebot, Verkaufsgespräch
to **place an order** einen Auftrag erteilen, eine Bestellung aufgeben
to **place demands on sb** Anforderungen an jdn stellen
pleasantries Höflichkeiten, Freundlichkeiten
pleased erfreut
pleased, to be ~ sich freuen
plug Stecker
to **plug in** einstecken
to **plummet** abstürzen, fallen
point of contact Ansprechpartner, Anlaufstelle
to **point out** darauf hinweisen
pointer Zeiger
policy Politik, Leitlinien
to **poll sb** jdn befragen
population Bevölkerung
portfolio Produktpalette
positioning statement Positionierungsaussage
potential potenziell

power outlet Stromanschluss, Steckdose
practice, best ~ beispielhafte Verfahren
precious wertvoll
preconception vorgefasste Meinung, Vorurteil
to **predict** vorhersagen
prediction Prognose
preferably am besten
preliminary Vorgeplänkel; vorläufig, vorhergehend
premier führend
prepayment Vorauszahlung
presence Anwesenheit, Präsenz
to **present** vorstellen, präsentieren
to **present sb with sth** jdm etw (als Geschenk) überreichen
presentation Präsentation
to **pressurize sb** *(BE)* jdn unter Druck setzen
to **pretend** so tun, als ob
pricing scheme Preismodell, Preisregelung, Preisgestaltung
pricing Preisgestaltung
primarily vorrangig, hauptsächlich
prime erstklassig
printers Druckerei
prior to vor, im Vorfeld von
procedure Verfahren
production facilities Produktionsanlagen
profile Profil, Image
projector, data ~ Beamer
to **prolong** verlängern
to **promise** versprechen
promising vielversprechend
to **promote sth** für etw Werbung machen
promotional Werbe-
promotional material Werbematerial
promotional price Aktionspreis, Sonderangebotspreis
promotional staff Promotion-Mitarbeiter
prompt umgehend, sofortig, prompt
to **proofread** Korrektur lesen
proposal Vorschlag
to **propose** vorschlagen
prospect potentielle/r Kunde/-in
prospective customer potentielle/r Kunde/-in
prosperous erfolgreich
to **protect** schützen
prototype Prototyp
proverb Sprichwort
to **provide** liefern, bieten, zur Verfügung stellen
provider Anbieter, Dienstleister
public transport öffentliche Verkehrsmittel
to **pull out of sth** sich von etw zurückziehen
purchasing manager Einkaufsleiter/in

push pin Drückerstift, Pinnwandnadel
pushy forsch, aufdringlich

Q

to **qualify** näher bestimmen
quality standards Qualitätsnormen, -anforderungen
quantity Menge
quarter Quartal
to **question** fragen, in Frage stellen

R

rack Ständer, Gestell
range Auswahl, Angebot, Palette
rapid schnell, rasch
rapport (gutes) Verhältnis
rate Gebühr, Preis, Satz; Rate
rating Bewertung, Einstufung
re betreffend, bezüglich
to **reach** erreichen
reality Wirklichkeit
reception Empfang
recipe Rezept
recipient Empfänger/in
to **reckon** glauben, denken
recognition Wiedererkennung, Anerkennung
to **recognize** erkennen
to **reconsider** überdenken
to **recruit** anwerben, gewinnen, einstellen
recruitment Anwerbung, Einstellung
red tape Bürokratie, Verwaltungsbürokratie, Papierkrieg
reference Bezug, Verweis, Erwähnung
to **refuse** sich weigern
to **regard sth as sth** etw für etw halten, etw für etw erachten
regarding bezüglich, betreffend
to **register** sich anmelden
to **regret** bedauern
regulatory interferences behördliche/staatliche Eingriffe
to **release** befreien, freistellen, entlassen
reliable zuverlässig
to **relieve sb** jdn ablösen
reluctant zurückhaltend, zögerlich
remarkably erstaunlich
to **remind sb of sth** jdn an etw erinnern
remnant Überbleibsel
remote entlegen
rental Miete, Miet-
to **replace** ersetzen, austauschen
to **represent** repräsentieren, vertreten, darstellen
to **request** anfordern, erbitten, bitten, wünschen
to **require** erfordern, verlangen
required erforderlich
requirement Vorschrift, Anspruch, Anforderung

to **reschedule** *(Termin)* verlegen, neu vereinbaren
research Forschung
residue, paint ~ Farbreste
respect, with ~ to hinsichtlich, betreffend
to **respond** antworten
responsible, to be ~ for sth für etw zuständig/verantwortlich sein.
responsible, to be held ~ for sth für etw haften
restricted beschränkt, begrenzt
restrictions, dietary ~ Ernährungsvorschriften, -einschränkungen
restrictions, territorial ~ Gebietsbeschränkungen
retail Einzelhandel
retailer Einzelhändler
to **rethink** überdenken
retrieval, call ~ Gesprächs-annahme, Gesprächsabruf
to **reveal** verraten
to **reveal oneself** sich zu erkennen geben
revenue Einkünfte
reverse side Rückseite
to **revise** überarbeiten, revidieren, korrigieren
to **revolutionize** revolutionieren
rid, to get ~ of sb/sth jdn/etw loswerden
rise Aufschwung, Anstieg
rise, on the ~ im Aufwind
to **rocket** in die Höhe schießen
ROI (return on investment) Rendite, Rentabilität
rope, to learn the ~s sich einarbeiten, etw in den Griff bekommen
rope stanchions Standabsperrung
roster, duty ~ Dienstplan
rough grob
row stand Reihenstand
row Reihe
royalties Lizenzgebühren
to **run sth** etw durchführen
to **run into sb** jdn treffen, jdm (zufällig) begegnen
to **run late** spät dran sein
rush, in a ~ in Eile

S

safety hazard Gefahrenquelle
safety standards Sicherheitsvorschriften
sales Vertrieb, Verkauf, Absatz
sales force Verkaufspersonal, Vertreterstab
sales manager Verkaufsleiter/in
sales operation Vertriebsniederlassung
sales report Verkaufsbericht
sales rep(resentative) Handelsvertreter/in, Vertriebs-/ Außendienstmitarbeiter/in
satisfactory zufriedenstellend

to **satisfy** befriedigen, erfüllen
savings Ersparnisse
scarce knapp
scene, behind the ~s hinter den Kulissen
schedule (Zeit-)Plan
scotch tape Klebeband, Tesafilm
screen Bildschirm
screwdriver Schraubenzieher
screw Schraube
secure sicher
to **secure** befestigen
security guard Wachmann, Sicherheitsbedienstete/r
security guarding Bewachung
security service Sicherheitsdienst
to **see to sth** sich um etw kümmern
senior position leitende Stellung
serial number Seriennummer
serious ernst, ernsthaft
seriously ernst, ernsthaft, im Ernst
service Dienstleistung
service, to be of ~ to sb jdm von Nutzen sein
to **set sth aside** etw erübrigen
to **set sth up** etw aufstellen
setting-up time Aufbauzeit
share Aktie
shelf, shelves Regal, Regale
shine, come rain or ~ in guten wie in schlechten Zeiten
shop, to talk ~ über Geschäfte reden
short and sweet kurz und bündig
to **shoulder sth** etw auf sich nehmen
show Messe, Ausstellung
showcase Ausstellung
to **shut down** abschalten, abstellen
to **sign** unterschreiben
to **sign up** sich anmelden
significance Bedeutung
to **simulate** simulieren
sink Spüle, Ausguss
site, on ~ vor Ort
sizeable beträchtlich, erheblich
to **sketch sth out** etw skizzieren, etw umreißen
skirted table Tisch mit bodenlanger Tischdecke
sleeping mat Isomatte
slot Zeitfenster
slump Einbruch, Krise, starker Rückgang
small and medium-sized businesses kleine und mittelständische Unternehmen
smoothly reibungslos, glatt
to **soar** in die Höhe schnellen, hochfliegen
socket *(BE)* Steckdose
soiled verschmutzt
sole Sohle
solely allein
solution Lösung

sophisticated hoch entwickelt, technisch ausgereift, durchdacht
to **sort sth out** etw in Ordnung bringen, etw klären
spare Reserve
to **speak up** lauter sprechen
speaker Redner/in, Vortragende/r
special conditions Sonderkonditionen
specialist Spezial-
specialist dealer Fachhändler
to **specialize in sth** sich auf etw spezialisieren
speech intellegibility Sprachverständlichkeit
to **speed up** beschleunigen
spite, in ~ of trotz
to **spot** entdecken
spotlight Scheinwerfer
spreadsheet Tabelle, Tabellen-kalkulationsprogramm
square meter Quadratmeter
stable stabil
staff Personal, Mitarbeiter
staff, cleaning ~ Reinigungskräfte
staffer Mitarbeiter/in
staffer, booth ~ Standmitarbeiter/in
stained fleckig
stand Stand
stand, corner ~ Eckstand
stand, end ~ Kopfstand
stand, island ~ Inselstand
stand, row ~ Reihenstand
stand engineering Standtechnik
stand rental Standmiete
standard, to meet ~s Ansprüche/ Maßstäbe erfüllen
standardization Normierung, Vereinheitlichung
standardized genormt, standardisiert
stand-up table, draped ~ Stehtisch mit Husse
state Zustand
state-of-the-art hochmodern, auf dem neuesten Stand der Technik
stationery Büromaterial
steamer Dampfgarer
steel pan Stahlpfanne
stool Hocker
to **store** lagern
strategy, entrance ~ Eintrittsstrategie, Zugangsstrategie
strategy, exit ~ Rückzugsstrategie
to **stress** betonen
stress test Belastungstest
to **stretch** strapazieren, belasten
strictly speaking genau genommen
to **strike** zuschlagen
to **strike up a conversation with sb** mit jdm ins Gespräch kommen
stroke of genius Geniestreich
to **stroll** schlendern
structure Konstruktion, Gestell
subconsciously unterbewusst

subscription   Abonnement, Vertrag
to **submit**   einreichen
subsidiary   Niederlassung
to **suggest**   vorschlagen, darauf hindeuten, erkennen lassen
to **suit sth**   zu etw passen
suited to   geeignet für, passend für
supplier   Lieferant, Zulieferer
support   Unterstützung, Dienst
supposed, to be ~ to do sth   etw tun sollen
sure, to make ~   dafür sorgen, gewährleisten, sicherstellen
to **surge**   stark ansteigen
to **surpass**   übersteigen
surveillance   Überwachung
survey   Umfrage, Studie
survival kit   Überlebenspaket/ -ausrüstung
to **sympathize**   nachempfinden, verstehen

T

table, draped stand-up ~   Stehtisch mit Husse
table, high ~   Stehtisch
table, skirted ~   Tisch mit bodenlanger Tischdecke
to **take sth down**   etw abbauen
to **take it further**   weitergehen
tailor-made   maßgeschneidert
to **talk shop**   über Geschäfte reden
tape   Band, Klebeband
target audience   Zielgruppe
target group   Zielgruppe
task   Aufgabe
technical specifications   technische Daten/Angaben
technician   Techniker/in
technology   Technik, Technologie
template   Schablone, Vorlage
temporarily   vorübergehend
tempted, to be ~ to do sth   versucht sein, etw zu tun
to **tend to do sth**   dazu neigen, etw zu tun
tent   Zelt
terms and conditions   Geschäftsbedingungen
terrain   Gelände
territorial restrictions   Gebietsbeschränkungen
ticket checking   Einlasskontrolle
tied up   beschäftigt
tight   eng
to **tighten up**   (Schraube) festdrehen, anziehen
time concept   Zeitvorstellung, Zeitverständnis
time frame   Zeitrahmen
token   Zeichen
ton   Tonne
tool   Werkzeug
toolkit   Werkzeugkasten
to **top sth**   etw übertreffen
top, over the ~   übertrieben
towel   Handtuch

toxic   giftig, toxisch
trade fair   (Handels-, Branchen-) Messe
trade fair discount   Messerabatt
trade show   (Branchen-)Messe
trade   Handel
trailer   Anhänger
to **transfer sth**   etw transportieren
trash   Abfall
travel expenses   Reisekosten
treadmill   Laufband
tremendous   enorm, ungeheuer
trivial   banal, trivial
to **turn out**   sich erweisen, sich herausstellen
to **turn up**   erscheinen, kommen
turnout   Beteiligung, Zulauf, (Publikums-)Andrang

U

unattended   unbeaufsichtigt
unavailable   nicht verfügbar
unbiased   unvoreingenommen, ohne Vorurteile
uncertainty   Unsicherheit, Ungewissheit
undecided   ungewiss
undisclosed   ungenannt, verdeckt
unforeseeable   unvorhersehbar
unique   einzigartig, einmalig
to **unload**   entladen
to **unplug**   ausstecken, entfernen
unpredictable   unvorhersehbar
unrivalled   konkurrenzlos, unübertroffen
unsanitary   unhygienisch
unsecured   unbefestigt
unsightly   unansehnlich
unusable   unbenutzbar
up, to be ~ to sth   etw vorhaben
up in the air   in der Schwebe, ungewiss
upcoming   bevorstehend, demnächst stattfindend
up-market   im oberen Marktsegment, gehoben, hochpreisig
upset   verärgert
urgent   dringend
utensils   Geräte, Utensilien
utilities   Versorgungseinrichtungen
utmost, of ~ importance   von allergrößter Bedeutung

V

valuable   wertvoll
value   Wert
value (for money), good/great ~   (sehr) preisgünstig, (sehr) preiswert
to **value**   schätzen, wertschätzen
valued   geschätzt
various   verschiedene
vehicle access   Zufahrt
vehicle   Fahrzeug
Velcro strips   Klettband
vendor   Verkäufer/in

venue   Veranstaltungsort
veteran, business ~   altgediente/r, erfahrene/r Geschäftsmann/-frau
view   Ansicht
virtual(ly)   virtuell
visitor management   Besucherlenkung, Besuchermanagement
visitor record form   Besuchererfassungsformular
visitor traffic   Besucherandrang
to **visualize**   sich ein Bild (von etw) machen
vital   unerlässlich

W

warehouse   Lager
warehouse management   Lagerverwaltung
waste   Abfall; (Zeit-, Geld-) Verschwendung
waste management   Abfallentsorgung
wastebasket (BE)   Abfalleimer, Papierkorb
waterfront   Hafen, Hafenviertel
way, to go out of one's ~   sich besondere Mühe geben, etw zu tun
weight   Gewicht
weird   seltsam, merkwürdig, eigenartig
wet grip   Nasshaftung
to **while away the time**   sich die Zeit vertreiben
Will do!   Wird gemacht!
willing   bereit, willens
wining and dining   mit Geschäftspartnern schick essen gehen
wiring   Elektroinstallation
wise   klug
to **wonder**   sich fragen
to **work sth out**   etw ausarbeiten
workload   Arbeitspensum
worries   Sorgen, Probleme
worth   wert, im Wert von
worthwhile, to be ~   sich lohnen
to **wow sb**   jdn begeistern, jdn umhauen
to **write sth up**   etw schreiben, etw entwerfen

Tracklist

Track	Title	Exercise	Running time
01	Title / Copyright		0:45
02	Unit 1	Warm-Up	1:45
03	Unit 1	Exercise 2	3:45
04	Unit 1	Exercise 10	1:21
05	Unit 1	Exercise 13	4:19
06	Unit 1	Exercise 14	1:49
07	Unit 2	Exercise 7	5:34
08	Unit 2	Exercise 11	4:57
09	Unit 2	Exercise 14	1:15
10	Unit 3	Warm-Up	3:47
11	Unit 3	Exercise 1	3:01
12	Unit 3	Exercise 4	3:18
13	Unit 4	Exercise 1	3:19
14	Unit 4	Exercise 2	1:21
15	Unit 4	Exercise 5	3:01
16	Unit 4	Exercise 6	0:57
17	Unit 4	Exercise 8	2:32
18	Unit 4	Exercise 10	1:05
19	Unit 4	Exercise 11	1:57
20	Unit 4	Exercise 14	3:43
21	Unit 5	Exercise 3	2:16
22	Unit 5	Exercise 8	3:22
23	Unit 5	Exercise 10	2:50
24	Unit 5	Exercise 12	2:31
25	Unit 5	Exercise 13	3:04
26	Unit 5	Exercise 17	3:36
27	Unit 6	Exercise 10	1:53
28	Business Challenge 1		0:57
29	Business Challenge 2		2:06
30	Business Challenge 3		0:30

Total running time   76:42 min.

Aufnahmestudio:
Clarity Studio Berlin

Aufnahmeleitung und Produzent:
Christian Schmitz

Tontechnik:
Pascal Thinius

SprecherInnen:
Shaunessy Ashdown, Andreas Goebel,
Urszula Goebel, Marianne Graffam, Steve Ellery,
Melissa Holroyd, Manon Kahle, Kevin McAlleer,
Helena Prince, Dharmander Singh, Darren Smith,
Ian H. Smith, Tomas Spencer, Clare Wigfall,
Ian Wood